Biotechnology and the Future
of World Agriculture

Biotechnology and the Future of World Agriculture

The Fourth Resource

Henk Hobbelink

Zed Books Ltd
London and New Jersey

Biotechnology and the Future of World Agriculture was first
published by Zed Books Ltd, 57 Caledonian Road,
London N1 9BU and 171 First Avenue, Atlantic Highlands,
New Jersey 07716, USA in 1991.

Cover designed by The Third Man
Typeset by Photosetting and Secretarial Services, Yeovil, Somerset
Printed and bound in the United Kingdom by Biddles Ltd,
Guildford and Kings Lynn

Library of Congress Cataloging-in-Publication Data

Hobbelink, Henk.
    Biotechnology and the future of world agriculture/Henk
Hobbelink.
        p.   cm.
    Includes bibliographical references.
    ISBN 0-86232-836-5. — ISBN 0-86232-837-3 (pbk.)
    1. Agricultural biotechnology — Forecasting.   I. Title.
S494.5.B563H63   1989   89-35866
631—dc20   CIP

British Library Cataloguing in Publication Data
Hobbelink, Henk
    Biotechnology and the future of world agriculture.
    1. Agriculture. Applications of biotechnology
    I. Title
    630

    ISBN 0-86232-836-5
    ISBN 0-86232-837-3 pbk

Contents

About GRAIN

Genetic Resources Action International (GRAIN) is an international foundation registered in Spain. GRAIN came into being out of a concern about the increasing loss of genetic diversity and its implications for agriculture worldwide. The overall objectives of GRAIN include:

To stimulate public awareness and concern about the vanishing resource base of agriculture.

To increase understanding of the structural causes behind genetic erosion, and its implications for the poor.

To stimulate activities and policies that lead to a better conservation of genetic diversity with a special focus on the interests of developing countries and small farmers.

To support the activities of public interest groups that are working on these issues and to facilitate communication and co-operation between them.

In order to realize these goals, GRAIN gathers and disseminates information, through publications and otherwise, brings public concern to the attention of policy makers, and lobbies for sustained activities and policies for the conservation of genetic diversity, and for the improvement of the situation of the poor. GRAIN also functions as the European contact point for the Seeds Action Network (SAN). *Seedling*, the bi-monthly newsletter of GRAIN, provides a regular information source on these issues. For information about our work, and for a full list of our publications, contact:

GRAIN
Apartado 23398, E-08080 Barcelona, Spain.
Telephone: (34-3) 412.11.89; Fax: (34-3) 302.21.18; Telex: 99767 E

About the Author

Henk Hobbelink was born in 1956 in the Netherlands. After receiving an M.Sc. in Agricultural Science and Entomology at the Agricultural University of Wageningen in 1982, he worked for two years in Amsterdam as Co-ordinator of the Agriculture in Developing Countries Programme of the Association for a New International Development Policy.

His lifelong interest in genetic diversity began with the research he conducted in 1978–79 on methods of biological pest control among small maize farmers in Peru. In 1984, he started working with the International Coalition for Development Action (ICDA) where he co-ordinated their Genetic Resources Programme. For the next five years he led this campaign, which grew to involve numerous NGOs and individuals in the struggle for the free exchange and proper conservation of genetic resources. He developed a special interest in, and knowledge of, the implications of the new biotechnologies for developing countries. In 1990, the ICDA Seeds Campaign became the separate and independent NGO, Genetic Resources Action International (GRAIN). Henk Hobbelink is its founder and first co-ordinator, as well as serving as co-editor of *Seedling*, its bi-monthly newsletter.

He is also the author of numerous articles, papers and reports on the subject of genetic resources and biotechnology, including *New Hope or False Promise? Biotechnology and Third World Agriculture* (1987), a booklet which has since been translated into eight different languages, including Japanese, Thai and Indonesian.

Abbreviations

ACES	Agency for Community Educational Services (Philippine NGO)
BIOTEC	National Institute of Biotechnology and Applied Microbiology (Philippines)
CBS	Cocoa Butter Substitutes
CENARGEN	National Research Centre of Genetic Resources (Brazil)
CGIAR	Consultative Group on International Agricultural Research
CIAT	International Centre for Tropical Agriculture
CIP	International Potato Institute (Peru)
CMA	Chemical Manufacturers' Association (US)
CMS	Cytoplasmic Male Sterility
CIMMYT	The International Centre for the Improvement of Maize and Wheat (Mexico)
DNA	deoxyribonucleic acid
EEC	European Economic Community
EMBRAPA	Brazilian Public Corporation for Agricultural Research
EPC	European Patent Convention
EPO	European Patent Office
FAO	Food and Agriculture Organization (UN)
GATT	General Agreement on Tariffs and Trade
GELPACEA	Group of Latin American and Caribbean Sugar Exporting Countries
HFCS	High Fructose Corn Syrup
HYV	High Yielding Varieties
IARC(s)	International Agricultural Research Centre(s)
ICA(s)	Interfirms Cooperation Agreement(s)
ICGEB	International Centre for Genetic Engineering and Biotechnology
ICRISAT	International Crop Research Institutes for the Semi-

	Arid Tropics
IITA	International Institute for Tropical Agriculture
ILO	International Labour Organization (Office) (UN)
ILRAD	International Laboratory for Research on Animal Diseases (Kenya)
IRRI	International Rice Research Institute
IUCN	International Union for the Conservation of Nature
KENGO	Kenya Energy and Environment Organizations
KNBTB	Dutch Organization of Catholic Farmers and Horticulturists
LDC	Lesser-developed Country
NBF	New Biotechnology Firm
NGO(s)	Non-governmental Organization(s)
NICs	Newly Industrializing Countries
OECD	Organization for Economic Co-operation and Development
OTA	Office of Technology Assessment (US)
PBR	Plant Breeders' Rights
PGI	Plant Genetics Incorporated (US)
PMA	Pharmaceutical Manufacturers' Association (US)
PRONAB	National Biotechnology Programme (Brazil)
R&D	research and development
SCO(s)	Single Cell Oil(s)
SCP	Single Cell Protein
SEARICE	Philippine based Community Organization
TNCs	Transnational Corporations
TRIPS	Trade Related Aspects of Intellectual Property Rights
UNCTAD	United Nations Conference on Trade and Development
UNIDO	United Nations Industrial Development Organization
UNRISD	United Nations Research Institute for Social Development
UPOV	Union for the Protection of New Varieties of Plants
US-ITC	US International Trade Commission
WIPO	World Intellectual Property Organization (UN)
ZSAN	Zimbabwe Seeds Action Network

Prologue

When Zed Books contacted me in 1988 to ask permission to republish *New Hope or False Promise?*, a booklet I had written a year earlier, my initial reaction was: great, but it needs updating first. What started off as updating a few tables and paragraphs, which I had thought of as taking a few weeks' work, almost turned into the writing of a new book on the same issue. In a process that took me almost two years – from accepting the idea to delivering the final product – I now can positively state that updating a book is more difficult than writing one. Still, I tremendously enjoyed doing it. The pace of breakthroughs in the new biotechnologies and the rapid changes in the industry are simply breathtaking. So is the process of trying to monitor them.

Biotechnology and the Future of World Agriculture, then, is a thoroughly expanded and updated version of *New Hope or False Promise?*. Readers of this earlier booklet will recognize bits and pieces of it in this book, but most of the material is drawn from more recent information sources. Some of the research done for this book has also resulted in articles for *Seedling*, which is the newsletter of GRAIN (Genetic Resources Action International), the organization with which I am working.

More than a product of my own research and thoughts, this book is the result of a collective effort. Numerous persons – too many to mention individually – participating in one way or the other in the different campaigns we are involved in, contributed often unwittingly in the preparation of this book. Renée Vellvé and David Cooper, my colleagues at GRAIN, were especially the source of substantial input. Not only did they do a tremendous job on the final editing but also assisted in much of the research and bits of the writing itself. In that sense the book is really a GRAIN effort. It goes without saying, however, that the views expressed and responsibility for any remaining errors are solely mine.

Last but not least there is Anna. Without her support to keep on going and her pressure to get it finished, this book would never have seen daylight.

Henk Hobbelink
Barcelona, 1991

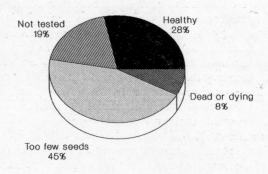

THE STATE OF THE US GENEBANK
ONLY 28% OF THE SEEDS FOUND HEALTHY

(in % of all seeds stored)

Not tested
19%

Healthy
28%

Dead or dying
8%

Too few seeds
45%

1. The Fourth Resource

'Solving a problem rather than worshipping the tool should be the goal.'
(M. S. Swaminathan, former Director, IRRI)[1]

Ask any agricultural scientist to list our natural resources, and the answer will probably be: 'soil, water and air'. Indeed, without any of these resources, no life would be possible. All three are under threat. The earth is losing fertile soil at a speed that seriously undermines agricultural production in many parts of the globe. There is a problem with water as well, as we all could witness when dramatic images of the African drought filled our TV screens. Apart from being polluted, the earth's atmosphere is losing its protective ozone layer while at the same time being filled up with greenhouse gases that threaten to change our global climate everywhere.

Yet there is a fourth, and equally important, resource which compared to the other three receives only limited attention. Genetic resources are the very foundation of all living beings. Genes are the physical support of hereditary information, coding for key characteristics of anything living, from the tiniest microbes to plants, animals and human beings. Diversity of genetic resources is a basic cornerstone for any effort to sustain or improve the performance of agricultural crops and animals. It is also a crucial prerequisite for natural ecosystems to respond to changing circumstances, now and in the future. Without a diverse mosaic of wild and locally bred plants and animals, together containing an immense wealth of genetic diversity, breeders would not have the raw material for their work. Still, despite the obvious importance of the fourth resource, much of the genetic diversity is now being lost at an unprecedented pace.

This is especially the case in developing countries where the vast majority of the planet's biological diversity is located. While in the upper regions of the Northern hemisphere subsequent ice ages slowed down the proliferation of life forms, the tropics and sub-tropics witnessed sustained evolutionary activity resulting in a rich wealth of species and varieties. It was also in those parts of the world that people first started domesticating the wild plants and animals around them, thus creating an impressive genetic mosaic of landraces and local breeds that best suited their needs. Today's global food supply rests on precisely that biological diversity in the fields, savannas and forests of what are now the developing countries.

Forces behind the erosion of this diversity are many. The bulldozers moving into tropical rainforests in search of timber are one. Large-scale projects to dam rivers and flood extensive areas of rich genetic diversity, and farmers in over-populated areas moving into fragile ecosystems, are just some of the others. Scientists estimate that we are currently losing at least one species a day. In the way we are managing our planet we may lose one million by the end of this century, and halfway through the next century one-quarter of all species might be lost.[2] But the loss of species is only one way of measuring how we are undermining our existence. Each species has numerous different and genetically distinct varieties, adapted to different ecosystems and climates. In agriculture, these are, to a large extent, man-made. For centuries, farmers selected, developed and maintained thousands of different plant and animal varieties, each of them responding to specific needs. When agricultural modernization schemes introduce new and uniform crop varieties into the farmers' fields – thus pushing into extinction numerous local varieties – much of this invaluable diversity is lost, forever. The irony of plant and animal breeding is that in this way it destroys the very building blocks on which the technology depends. In the words of Professor Garrison Wilkes of the University of Massachusetts it is analogous to taking stones from a building's foundation to repair the roof.[3]

The recognition of the danger of the erosion of our food base has prompted reactions, especially in the field of plant genetic resources. The first efforts were mainly focused on collection of seed samples for storage and use in breeding programmes. The world's first major genebank resulted from the extensive collection missions in many parts of the world directed by a Russian scientist, Vavilov. Genebanks are essentially vast refrigerators where seed samples are stored under controlled humidity and temperature conditions. In the 1950s, the USA established its National Seed Storage Laboratory (NSSL) now one of the world's largest genebanks. Other industrialized nations followed suit, and in the 1960s the International Agricultural Research Centres started their research, which included the setting up of several crop-specific genebanks.

It did not take long before questions were raised about the approach of using high-tech genebanks to store and conserve genetic diversity for future generations. Seeds lose viability if they are not grown out regularly. Cold storage itself can affect the genetic material in the seed, and improper management of the genebank endangers much of the alleged diversity in storage. The issue was first vigorously raised by NGOs concerned about the future of the food supply, but later also taken up by scientists from within the system. Dr William L. Brown, Chairman of Pioneer Hi-Bred, the world's largest seed company, thinks that we could be losing more genetic diversity in genebanks than in the field.[4] Donald Duvick, from the same company, is of the opinion that the neglect of conservation of genetic resources in the US is 'inexcusable, not only in regard to our national obligations, but also in regard to our responsibility to the entire world.'[5]

A recent evaluation of the seed collection in the central US genebank in Fort Collins disclosed alarming figures. Of all stored seed samples only 28% have been tested and found healthy. The rest of the collection has not been tested for at least five years, contains too few seeds to risk testing, or is already dead.[6] (See Graph 1.1.) Yet this is the place where the future of agriculture is supposed to be conserved. The US genebank at Fort Collins is not the only one in poor shape. The vast majority of the world's genebanks might fall below generally accepted safety standards, as indicated in a survey by the International Board for Plant Genetic Resources (IBPGR).[7] M. Goodman, of the North Carolina State University, prefers the word 'genemorgues' rather than banks and denounces the false sense of security that is being given: 'The existence of so many "seed morgues" has reassured the public, most administrators and virtually all politicians . . . that the world's germplasm is being carefully managed.'[8]

The fourth resource is not only threatened by erosion, but also by economic control and political power-play. The majority of the world's genebanks are under control of the industrialized nations, while virtually all the genetic diversity originates from the fields and forests of developing countries. This sparked-off a heated debate in several international fora, but especially in the Food and Agricultural Organization of the UN (FAO). Prompted by the skewed situation in which developing nations are the main donors of this raw material for plant breeding, while the industrialized countries claim ownership over it through intellectual property rights, the Third World started to demand free access to genetic resources and a more equitable conservation system. The debate resulted in an intergovernmental FAO Commission and an agreement to consider plant genetic resources as the common heritage of humanity, which should be properly conserved and freely exchanged.

While such developments are truly encouraging, the reality of the situation is not. The same resource that the world's nations, meeting in plush FAO conference rooms, denominated 'common heritage of mankind', is also the raw material for a multi-billion dollar industry. Once, seed was entirely in the domain of the farmer. It was both product and means of production, as part of the harvest was retained for the following year's sowing. Now, seeds and genetic resources have increasingly become a commodity. A peculiar commodity as it is obtained from the South at no cost. Starting with the hybridization of maize, which increased yields but made it useless for on-farm reproduction, the seed as a means of production became increasingly undermined. Now, hybrids are available for several crops, and industry is working hard to extend this in-built protection to them all. When industrialized countries started allowing for intellectual property rights on plant varieties in the 1960s, the 'commodification' of the seed was further accelerated.[9] Now, almost touching the end of the century, we stand at another threshold: genes, the very building blocks of life, are themselves becoming a commodity.

This book is about the technologies that make the commodification of the fourth resource possible. It is also about how they affect agriculture, especially in developing countries. One can hardly open a popular scientific magazine these days without finding exciting articles on the potential blessings of the newly emerging biotechnologies. Some of these articles stress the promise of yield increases through genetic engineering. Others tell us about super-plants that could produce their own fertilizers and pesticides, thus reducing the need for costly and harmful agro-chemicals, or about plants that could be grown on poor soils on which agriculture is difficult if not impossible. Yet others point to the huge possibilities of engineering micro-organisms which could attack their relatives that damage crops. The list of possibilities seems endless and promises great advantages, especially for agriculture in developing countries which so desperately need to produce more food without destroying the resource base.

The excitement over the possibilities of the bio-revolution remind us of the mood when the first results of another revolution started to reach the fields of the farmers in the Third World: the so-called 'Green Revolution'. 'Miracle seeds', developed at the International Agricultural Research Centres, raised hopes and offered the promise of reaching one of the most important goals of developing countries: the ability to feed themselves. Now, a few decades and numerous studies later, the proponents and opponents are still debating the consequences. The proponents point to the substantial increases in food production as a result of the Green Revolution, turning countries like India and Indonesia from food importers to food exporters. Opponents stress the socio-economic implications and the environmental costs: the increased gap between agricultural production and food consumption at the local level, the marginalization of small farmers, and the environmental degradation caused by the new farming techniques. While proponents wave statistics on, for example, increased wheat production in India, others show that a quarter of India's population still suffers famine and show that the increased production took place at the cost of crops traditionally used by the poor. They also point to the growing dependence on the chemical industries for the supply of the Revolution's indispensable agro-inputs.

Probably both camps are right. The Green Revolution did increase food production substantially in some developing countries. But it did so at a considerable cost: the position of the poor in those countries and the dependence on expensive inputs from outside. Perhaps the most important lesson to be learned from the Green Revolution is that technology as such is not a solution, but a tool. A very special tool with a degree of built-in direction towards a certain type of development. Its success depends only in part on its scientific quality; it also depends on the way it is made and the circumstances in which it is developed and used, the interests of those who introduce it and the situation of those to whom it is directed.

Although some of the possibilities of the new biotechnologies might be very much exaggerated, the potentials are breathtaking; and billions of dollars are currently being poured into research and development to make them possible. A true 'biotech race' is taking place among the main industrialized blocs. Although the Third World is largely an outsider in this race, it certainly will not be an outsider when it comes to the impact. As with the Green Revolution, the question is not *whether* biotechnology will reach the poor, but *how* and *with what consequences*. Biotechnology not only offers a powerful tool to improve agricultural production, but also can provide the means to increase the degree of monopoly control over agricultural production. While general awareness of the impact of the Green Revolution came a decade after the impact was felt, with the bio-revolution there may be still time to raise some of the crucial points now, namely how should the technology be developed, by whom and for whose benefit?

Notes and references

1. M. S. Swaminathan, 'Biotechnology Research and Third World Agriculture', in *Science*, Vol. 218, 3 December 1982, p. 972.

2. Norman Myers (ed.) *The Gaia Atlas of Planet Management*, PAN Books, London, 1985, p. 154.

3. Quoted in ibid, p. 156.

4. Ibid, p. 37. Brown referred specifically to maize germplasm.

5. Quoted in Major M. Goodman, 'What genetic and germplasm stocks are worth conserving?' Paper presented at the AAAS symposium. San Francisco, 16 January, 1989.

6. Findings of a three-month investigation of Associated Press (AP), reported in *Agri-News*, Vol. 14, No. 14, USA, 6 April 1989. See also *Seedling*, ICDA Seeds Campaign, Vol. 6, No. 5, October 1989, pp. 2–3.

7. See Fowler et al., 'The Laws of Life', in *Development Dialogue*, No. 1/2, Uppsala, 1988, pp. 281–6.

8. M. Goodman, 1989, op. cit.

9. Jack Kloppenburg, *First the Seed*, Cambridge University Press, Cambridge, USA, 1988 provides a good discussion on the 'commodification' of the seed.

2. Agriculture in Crisis

'A farmer is one who is asked to feed the world. . . . in exchange for enough money to starve his family.'
(Johny Hart)[1]

The report of the World Commission on Environment and Development put it all in one volume. Published in 1987, and better known as the Brundtland report, *Our Common Future*[2] analyses some of the more structural causes of underdevelopment and environmental degradation. There are more hungry people in the world today than ever before in human history and their number is growing; so is the total number of people inhabiting our globe. The gap between the rich and the poor is increasing, both in North-South terms and within countries. With repayments of debt, which now top the $1 trillion mark, and a further deterioration in terms of trade, the Third World poor are actually – in net terms – pouring money into the industrialized North at a rate of $50 billion a year or more.[3] This negative flow of resources is perverse and defies all economic logic – it is development assistance in reverse. To make a bad situation worse, developing countries are being increasingly excluded from international trade. While the Third World held 28% of global trade in 1980, this share had dropped to 19% in 1986,[4] and has remained at about that level since.

Developing countries are mired within the debt crisis, trade barriers, falling commodity prices, population growth and environmental degradation. They have few alternatives to exporting more cash crops at ever decreasing prices, despite the consequences for the environment and their people. The ones who lose out the most are, as always, the poor.

The soil and water crisis

If the Brundtland report made one thing clear, it is that we are destroying, at an incredible rate, the very base of our capability to produce. The earth is losing soil at a pace which is threatening agricultural production the world over. By the late 1970s, soil erosion exceeded soil formation on about one-third of US cropland. In India, soil erosion affects over one-quarter of all land under cultivation. Globally, over one-third of the earth's land area suffers from some form of desertification, both in the North and in the South. At least six million hectares of valuable crop land is irreversibly lost in this way each year. The UN's Food and Agriculture Organization calculates that in the long run the Third World alone will lose over 500 million hectares of rainfed cropland because of soil erosion and degradation.[5] To get some grasp of dimensions, this is more than twice the area now planted to rice and wheat in the entire Third World,[6] almost four times the size of all of India's arable land, and over three times all agricultural land in the USA.

Most of this soil destruction is a direct result of human activity in the form of inappropriate agricultural modernization schemes and deforestation for logging and food production. Desertification is not confined to the Third World. Take a walk on a dry and windy spring day in the potato fields of Groningen, a northern province of the Netherlands. You will most likely find yourself in the midst of a dust storm, blowing away substantial parts of the top soil. Years of intensive soil treatment with the world's most powerful biocides to make continuous potato production possible, are turning this once so fertile province into a barren desert.

Even where the soil is not literally being blown away because of erosion and desertification, it is often being ruined in other ways. In what has been called '*the greatest threat to sustainable food security*',[7] the earth's soil is being crippled by salinization, alkalinization and water-logging. Salinization and water-logging are to a large extent induced by modern irrigation schemes and therefore often occur on the most fertile soils. When large quantities of water loaded with minerals, salts and other substances are used through irrigation on soils of poor drainage, the water table comes closer to the surface, evaporates and leaves behind an ever increasing concentration of salts. Additionally, a high water table prevents plant roots from penetrating deep enough into the soil. Both processes render land useless for agriculture. It is estimated that half of all existing irrigation projects suffer from these intoxication processes, forcing some 10 million hectares of irrigated land to be abandoned annually.[8]

In India alone, ten million hectares of irrigated cropland are water-logged or saline, resulting in productivity losses of 20% or more.[9] In the Sahel, the rate at which irrigated land is abandoned because of these problems matches almost exactly the rate at which new irrigation schemes are introduced.[10] The other side of the coin of water-logging is water-mining. The explosive increase in the use of electric tubewells to pump water to the surface in many parts of the Third World has caused water tables to fall in the areas supplying the irrigation water. In many parts of the world this has already turned many millions of hectares of fertile soil into unproductive wasteland.

Decades of intensive use of chemical fertilizer, heavy machinery and pesticides have also degraded the soil. In industrialized countries, groundwater in many regions is severely polluted with either chemical pesticides or nitrates and phosphates. Many European farmers are now faced not only with milk and crop quotas, but also with quotas on the amount of natural and artificial fertilizers they are allowed to put on the land, as the authorities desperately try to turn the tide.

The soil and water crises are intimately interlinked. What they have in common is that they are largely man-made and result from over-exploitation due to farming methods based on a reductionist approach to the use of natural resources. They turn two renewable resources *par excellence* – soil and water – into non-renewable ones. Together they form one of the most serious threats to agricultural production everywhere.

The productivity crisis

In what seems to be meant as a final response to the Green Revolution critics, the World Bank published in 1988 a major report on the implications of this all-encompassing agricultural modernization scheme.[11] It was drawn up by the Consultative Group on International Agricultural Research (CGIAR), which is the umbrella body for various research centres that spearheaded the Green Revolution. Their message is: yes, we made some mistakes in the early years of the Green Revolution, but we learned from them and are now heading in the right direction. The report, based on no less than 26 country and sectoral studies, concludes that a little less than 50% of the Third World's wheat fields and almost 60% of its rice fields are now sown with the Green Revolution varieties, together covering some 125 million hectares. It shows that, since the early 1960s, total wheat and rice production in the Third World increased by over 70%, resulting in $50 billion extra output. Quoting impressive yield increases due to the use of the High Yielding Varieties (HYV), the authors conclude that both small and large farmers are using them and that small farmers even tend to get more yield from the new seeds than their more resource-endowed neighbours. The report argues that the HYVs do better than their traditional relatives even without the use of fertilizer, and that resistance to pests and diseases has been greatly improved in the modern varieties.

But not all studies have found such impressive yield increases from the Green Revolution. In 1977, the Asian Development Bank concluded that

> The Green Revolution is not providing the expected impetus to production . . . The growth rate in rice yield between 1963–67 and 1971–75 was less than 1.5 percent per annum for South and Southeast Asia as a

whole, and below one percent for several countries.[12]

This observation has been confirmed by many other researchers later. Pierre Spitz talks about disappointing progress in rice production in India.[13] His analysis is that the Green Revolution in that country was largely a 'wheat revolution', and points out that an important part of the increase in wheat output was achieved at the cost of the area sown to pulses – the 'poor person's meat' and the main source of protein for many small farmers. Also, the acreage sown to local oilseeds diminished considerably. Graph 2.1 shows how this process took place in the Punjab, one of the focus areas of India's Green Revolution. Ademar Romeiro wonders why there is increasing food scarcity in Brazil with two and a half times more agricultural land and one-fifth of the population of India, while at the same time huge modernization schemes are restructuring Brazil's agriculture.[14] Vandana Shiva shows that the Green Revolution is actually destroying agricultural productivity at the local level and denounces 'the crisis mind' behind it.[15] And virtually all studies agree that Africa has been completely left out of this 'miracle' development.

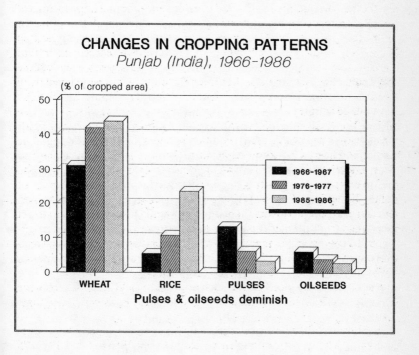

CHANGES IN CROPPING PATTERNS
Punjab (India), 1966-1986

(% of cropped area)

Legend:
- 1966-1967
- 1976-1977
- 1985-1986

WHEAT   RICE   PULSES   OILSEEDS

Pulses & oilseeds deminish

Apart from the statistics-war about the yield increases actually achieved with the Green Revolution technology, there is even more concern about how sustainable the alleged production increases are. One of the Green Revolution's success stories is the Philippines, home of the International Rice Research Institute (IRRI) which was established in the early 1960s. IRRI's Green Revolution technology, with the new rice varieties at its heart, quickly spread to the farmers' fields resulting in the doubling of the average rice yields of the country. The CGIAR claims that between 1968 and 1977 the modern rice varieties in the Philippines out-yielded their traditional counterparts by 30%.[16] By 1977, President Marcos was proud to announce the country's self-sufficiency in this staple crop. The Philippines began exporting rice rather than importing. The first official dissonant note, however, came from the abovementioned study of the Asian Development Bank and subsequent publications of the United Nations' Research Institute for Social Development (UNRISD),[17] along with many different NGO reports. Where yields rose dramatically, it was often at the cost of expensive chemical inputs and sophisticated irrigation schemes. Due to the increased costs, peasants' incomes began declining until they could no longer afford the necessary inputs, and the growth rate of rice production subsequently began to drop in the early 1980s. By 1984, the Philippines again began importing rice.[18] Was this despite or because of the fact that 80% of the country's rice acreage had been turned over to HYVs in the meanwhile?

Through the looking glass

The impact of the Green Revolution can be explained only in part by looking at national and international production statistics. The real impact took place at the local level, and it is precisely there where the production crisis becomes most apparent. This has been the level that has often been overlooked by the Green Revolution scientists, who are more used to turning their magnifying glasses on plants than on people's communities.

Staying with our example of the Philippines, ACES, a Filipino NGO focusing on community organization, conducted a survey among small farmers in four different villages on their experience with the Green Revolution varieties of rice developed by IRRI. The survey was in an area which had been a special focus of the Green Revolution: all interviewed farmers had shifted completely from traditional to IRRI rice varieties between 1970 and 1981. The results showed that despite yield increases of over 70%, the farmers' real income had dropped by as much as 50%.[19] This dramatic decrease in income was caused on the one hand by the price farmers got for their rice being cut in half and on the other by a tremendous increase in the amount and the cost of the inputs required for IRRI varieties. Graph 2.2 shows that between 1970 and 1981 the cost of manual weeding doubled, the use of herbicides jumped from zero to 10% of all input costs and the use and costs of pesticides and fertilizer more than tripled. All together this meant an increase of the cost for inputs of no less than 360%! The falling income, combined with the ever-growing need for external inputs, resulted in the farmers' increasing indebtedness. ACES later broadened its research into other areas of the Philippines with comparable results.

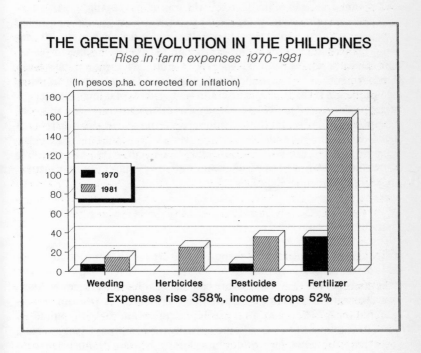

THE GREEN REVOLUTION IN THE PHILIPPINES
Rise in farm expenses 1970-1981

(In pesos p.ha. corrected for inflation)

Legend: ■ 1970 ▨ 1981

Categories: Weeding, Herbicides, Pesticides, Fertilizer

Expenses rise 358%, income drops 52%

Looking at local communities and their agricultural production systems, one starts realizing that national production statistics of individual crops completely overlook a substantial part of production that is important at the local level. Vandana Shiva, in her study on the role of women in Indian ecology, perhaps best explains this:

> In the context of diverse outputs from the farm, the HYVs were not really high yielding even under the best conditions. They appeared high yielding because a whole system of cropping that provided diverse food to man, animals and the earth was reduced to the output of a single crop.[20]

She continues to explain how many local farming practices, based on centuries of experience with the local situation, evolve around a complex system in which plant and animal production are inherently tied together and in which soil and water management are a crucial part of sustained production. In the Green Revolution's focus on single commodity output, such balanced systems are disturbed, resulting in productivity collapses, soil degradation and over-exploitation of water and mineral resources.

In many countries of the Third World, multiple cropping, in which several crops are produced together on the same field, has proved to be a highly efficient and sustainable way of producing food and a whole series of other products. In India, farmers intercrop sorghum and wheat with different pulses, and mixtures involving up to eight crops are not uncommon.[21] Farmers in Latin America grow maize and beans together, in a system where the maize functions as a stalk for the beans. Different systems of intercropping provide for a balanced use of soil fertility and often increase the humus content of the soil. Also, multiple cropping patterns provide for greater protection against pests and diseases as the variability in the field reduces the likelihood of the massive pest outbreaks that occur in the uniform single crop systems of the Green Revolution. In chapter 9 such farmers' practices are discussed in more detail.

The hidden harvest

Of course, when single-crop output is measured to show productivity increases of the new varieties, the *loss* of the associated crops, which were originally part of the system, is not calculated. This loss can be considerable. In south India intercropped sorghum provided – apart from the sorghum – some 70 kilogrammes of different pulses and 10 kilogrammes of local oilseeds per acre.[22] The disappearance of these intercropping systems, with the introduction of new sorghum varieties bred for monoculture conditions, considerably reduced the availability of protein and fat sources at the local level. Additionally, the new dwarf varieties reduced the amount of straw available, thus upsetting the plant/animal/soil balance of local agricultural production systems.

Also not calculated in the alleged super-harvests of the Green Revolution is the loss of other food sources when farmers turn to monoculture and the associated chemicals. Rene Salazar, working with SEARICE – a Philippine based community organization – explains how increased pesticide use is virtually destroying a widespread resource base whereby fish from the paddy fields provide protein-rich food for rural families.[23] Snails, frogs and birds from the paddy fields also used to provide food for farmer households. All of these are disappearing as irrigation water is contaminated with toxic pesticides and fertilizers. A related problem is the impact of pesticides on the health of buffaloes, in many ways 'the small farmer's tractor'. In the ACES survey cited above, 20% of the farmers complained about the frequency with which pesticide poisoning causes the death of these invaluable animals.[24]

Yet another example of lost production (lost for the farmers, but normally also lost in production statistics) is the disappearance of associated 'weeds' and wild plants in the farmers' fields when herbicides are used to keep the monoculture as mono as possible. Filipino farmers derived substantial quantities of protein-rich food from these 'weeds' and so do Indian women farmers when singling out *Bathua* plants for consumption during manual weeding. The same women used another weed as raw material for weaving mats and baskets. These mats and baskets, sold at the local market, formed an important additional source of income for the rural women. The monocultural mind considers these plants as unwanted pests and uses herbicides to kill them off. In this way, not only supplementary protein sources are lost to the rural poor, but also the little extra income for women from selling mats and baskets. It is interesting how Western language already indicates our misunderstanding of these plants which grow in association with specific crops. Weeds are labelled as *unkraut* in German and as *malas hierbas* in Spanish, both terms having 'bad' as the common denominator.

Not only 'weeds', but also wild plants gathered from the proximity of cultivated areas, traditionally provide farmers with a precious source of vitamin-rich greens and dietary supplements. In Third World countries, collection of edible wild species is common practice in the pre-harvest season and a major resource in times of food shortage. East African farmers depend on various kinds of spinach, on locust beans, baobab leaves and other wild plants carefully maintained to palliate nutrition and supply problems. Wild plants are also critical components of traditional health-care products in many developing countries. Indications of the destructive toll chemical biocides have taken against these herbaceous sources of food and health are also hard to find in the impressive yield-increase statistics.

When, then, the masters of the Green Revolution calculate the enormous increases in wheat and rice production in the Third World and the resulting $50 billion increased value of these crops since 1965,[25] many relevant figures are completely overlooked. The first question which has to be raised is how many billions of dollars in associated crop production were actually lost when farmers shifted to monoculture to make this increased value possible. A second question relates to the extra costs of such production systems, not only for the farmer in the form of extra chemical inputs but also for society in general in the form of environmental degradation. Finally, a very legitimate question is where the alleged $50 billion ended up. Certainly not in the pockets of the vast majority of Filipino and many other farmers, as we have seen above.

The problems not addressed

A surprising and probably unintended criticism of the limitations of the Green Revolution comes from one of its main donors: the Rockefeller Foundation.[26] The Foundation has launched a major rice biotechnology programme in which IRRI is playing a major role. Having learned from the Green Revolution, the Foundation wants to select sound criteria for priority setting. It looked at the main research problems in rice-growing and ordered them by importance. The problems were weighted according to relevance for poor farmers and impact on the environment, and put against the likelihood that new technologies could offer solutions. To get an idea of the main problems, the views of scientists from within the system were surveyed. This resulted in a list of 24 insect pests, 16 diseases, eight soil problems, eight water and temperature problems and 12 other problems that rice production faces. The problems were then analysed in relation to the extent that Green Revolution technology had paid attention to them and/or found solutions. The results are given in Table 2.1.

Table 2.1
Problems in rice and the Green Revolution response

Problem type	Tot.	ES	EU	IS	IN
Insect pests	24	1	3	6	14
Diseases	16	2	0	7	7
Soil problems	8	0	0	0	8
Water & temperature	8	0	0	5	3
Other problems	12	2	1	2	7
Total	**68**	**5**	**4**	**20**	**39**
%	100	7	6	30	57

Note: ES = effectively controlled and sustainable
EU = effectively controlled but not sustainable
IS = substantially researched but ineffective
IN = ineffective because no substantial research done

Source: R. W. Herdt, 'Equity considerations in setting priorities of Third World rice biotechnology research', in *Development*, special issue on biotechnology, Society for International Development (SID), No. 4, 1987, Rome, pp. 19–26.

The outcome of this Rockefeller survey is remarkable. Green Revolution scientists admit that for nearly 90% of the main problems in rice-growing no effective solution has been found. For only five out of the 68 problems listed were there sustained and effective solutions, while another four problems were effectively addressed but only for a limited time. Most of the major problems never have been seriously researched at all.

Biotechnology, the solution?

Biotechnology is often heralded as the tool to correct the problems and shortcomings of the Green Revolution. Talk of new pest, drought, frost and stress resistant plants, especially relevant for small farmers, dominates virtually every conference on the matter. If one assesses that a main problem of the Green Revolution was its emphasis on crops rather than on farmers and their sophisticated farming systems, one should ask whether the new biotechnologies will help to redirect this focus. This new set of technologies opens up huge possibilities to penetrate much deeper into the molecular structure of the plant and its genetic components. While this offers a tremendous potential for crop improvement itself, it does not necessarily promise a type of research that takes the farmer as a starting point while reversing the current top-down approach to agricultural development. In the midst of the soil and water crisis, biotechnology's solution to salinization points to salt tolerant plants, while desertification is handled with research on drought resistant crops. Such solutions are very appealing but what of the factors that cause the problems in the first place? Indeed, as scientists search more intensively in their laboratories to find even more miracle remedies, the current top-down approach might be reinforced rather than reversed. Even at the plant level, as we have seen with the Rockefeller survey cited above, the shortcomings of the Green Revolution are only in part technological. Much more numerous are the problems that have never been seriously addressed. Will the bio-revolution try to find solutions for farming problems which were never seriously looked at before?

Finally, there is a problem with interference. While the International Agricultural Research Centres (IARCs) were the lonely protagonists of the Green Revolution, the biotechnology revolution is eyed by a plethora of actors as highly promising territory. As we shall see in following chapters, this is especially the case for transnational corporations in the industrialized North. Apart from competition for the technology, there will be a competition for the market. This is likely to trigger off a whole series of negative implications for developing countries, which in many cases might prove to offset most of the possible benefits. In a much used and highly illustrative table (Table 2.2) originally drawn up by researchers at Cornell University in the USA, the Green and bio-revolutions are compared. It shows the tremendous scale on which the bio-revolution operates, compared to the Green Revolution. Perhaps more importantly, it points to the 'side-effects' of a technology being developed almost exclusively by and for the industrialized nations. These problematic, indirect effects might prove to be the main ones for developing countries if research priorities and international structures are not drastically reformulated.

Table 2.2
Comparing the Green Revolution and biorevolution

Characteristics	Green Revolution	Biorevolution
Crops affected	Wheat, rice, maize	Potentially all crops, including vegetables, fruits, agro-export crops (e.g. oil-palm, cocoa, etc.) and speciality crops (spices, etc.)
Other sectors affected	None	Pesticides, animal products, pharmaceuticals, processed food products, energy, mining, warfare
Territories affected	Some developing countries	All areas; all nations; all locations, including marginal lands (characterized by drought, salinity, aluminium toxicity, etc.)
Development of technology and dissemination	Largely public or quasi-public sector. IARC R&D around $100	Largely private sector, especially transnational corporations. R&D runs into billions of dollars
Proprietary considerations	Plant breeders rights and patents generally not relevant	Genes, cells, plants and animals patentable as well as the techniques to produce them
Capital costs of research	Relatively low	Relatively high for some techniques, relatively low for others
Access to information	Relatively easy, due to public policy of IARCs	Restricted, due to privatization and proprietary considerations
Research skills required	Conventional plant breeding and parallel agricultural sciences	Molecular and cell biology expertise plus conventional plant breeding skills
Crop vulnerability	High-yielding varieties relatively uniform, thus increasing genetic vulnerability	Crop propagation through tissue culture produces genetically exact copies which can increase vulnerability even more
'Side-effects'	Increased monoculture and use of farm chemicals, marginalization of small farmer. Ecological degradation	Crop substitution replacing Third World exports; herbicide tolerance; increasing use of chemicals; engineered organisms might affect environment; further marginalization of small farmer

Source: Martin Kenney, Frederick Buttel, 'Biotechnology: Prospects and Dilemmas for Third World Development', in *Development and Change,* Sage, London/Beverly Hills/New Delhi, Vol. 16, 1985, p. 70. Adapted by author.

Notes and references

1. Quoted in R. Modina, A. Ridao, *IRRI Rice: The Miracle That Never Was*, ACES Foundation, Quezon City, 1987.

2. World Commission on Environment and Development (WCED), *Our Common Future*, Oxford University Press, Oxford, 1987.

3. The World Bank's preliminary estimate for 1989 is $51.6 billion. In *World Debt Tables 1989–1990*, Vol. I, Table 2, World Bank, Washington, December 1989, p. 9.

4. Susan George, *A Fate Worse than Debt*, Penguin Books, London 1988, p. 73.

5. All data on erosion in this paragraph from WCED, 1987, op. cit., p. 125.

6. Total rice and wheat area in Third World calculated at 228 million hectares in 1983. In J. R. Anderson et al. *Science and Food, the CGIAR and its Partners*, World Bank, Washington, 1988, pp. 19–20.

7. WCED, *Food 2000*, A Report to the World Commission on Environment and Development, Zed Books, London, 1987, p. 62.

8. Ibid.

9. Estimates from B. Vohra, quoted by R. N. Roy, 'Trees: Appropriate tools for water and soil management' in B. Glaeser (ed.), *The Green Revolution Revisited*, Allen & Unwin, London, 1987, p. 115.

10. Lloyd Timberlake, *Africa in Crisis*, Earthscan, London, 1985, p. 79.

11. J. R. Anderson et al., 1988, op. cit.

12. Asian Development Bank. 'Asian Agriculture Survey 1976', Manila, 1977. Quoted in R. Modina, A. Ridao, 1987, op. cit., pp. 15–16.

13. Pierre Spitz, 'The Green Revolution Re-examined in India', in B. Glaeser (ed.), 1987, op. cit., pp. 56–76.

14. Ademar Romeiro, 'Alternative Developments in Brazil', in B. Glaeser (ed.), 1987, op. cit., pp. 79–110.

15. Vandana Shiva, *Staying Alive*, Kali for Women, Delhi, 1988 and Zed Books, London, 1989.

16. J. R. Anderson et al., 1988, op. cit., p. 28.

17. See for example Andrew Pearse, *Seeds of Plenty, Seeds of Want*, UNRISD, Geneva, 1980. UNRISD drew up several other studies on the impact of the Green Revolution.

18. Cunnington Putzel, *Gaining Ground: Agrarian Reform in the Philippines*, War on Want, London, 1989, p. 30.

19. R. Modina, A. Ridao, 1987, op. cit., pp. 35–42.

20. Vandana Shiva, 1989, op. cit., p. 124.

21. Pierre Spitz, 1987, op. cit., p. 66.

22. Vandana Shiva, 1989, op. cit., p. 124.

23. Rene Salazar, personal communication, April 1989, Uppsala, Sweden.

24. R. Modina, A. Ridao, 1987, op. cit., p. 54.

25. J. R. Anderson et al., 1988, op. cit., p. 29.

26. See R. W. Herdt, 'Equity Considerations in Setting Priorities of Third World Rice Biotechnology Research', in *Development*, special issue on biotechnology, Society of International Development (SID), 1987, No. 4, Rome, 1987, pp. 19–26.

3. The Tools

' Why trouble to make compounds yourself when a bug will do it for you?'
(Biologist J. B. S. Haldane, 1929)[1]

People have known for thousands of years that there are mechanisms that govern inheritance. Family resemblances could not be merely coincidental. Farmers also realized this long ago, when selecting crops and animals with desired characteristics for further reproduction. But the mechanism of how these characteristics are passed on from generation to generation has been understood only relatively recently. The first important contribution to this understanding was provided by the Austrian monk and botanist Gregor Mendel. From 1857 he spent many hours over several years in the gardens of his monastery, cross-breeding different pea varieties and trying to understand how traits such as colour and height were passed on to subsequent generations. Mendel pointed to 'hereditary factors' present in each of the parents, and was able to show that such factors do not blend when coming together in the offspring, but segregate. Sadly for Mendel, nobody took notice of his work and he died in 1884 without the slightest idea that his findings would, much later, form the very basis of plant and animal breeding and the science of genetics in general.

During the first half of this century many important improvements were made in the use of microbes for industrial production. But it was only in the 1940s that a Canadian doctor, Oswald Avery, established that the 'hereditary factors' Mendel had pointed to are located on the DNA (deoxyribonucleic acid). He and his colleagues managed to transfer DNA from one micro-organism to another, thus proving that the hereditary information is stored on it. This laid the basis for answering the questions of the 'why' and 'how' at breathtaking speed. In 1953, Watson and Crick unravelled the three-dimensional structure of DNA, a double helix, each composed of chains of four different chemical bases. Later, it was found that the DNA's bases in groups of three – each called a codon – form a code, and that several of them together – a gene – form the instructions for building a protein. By the mid-1960s the entire genetic code of DNA had been deciphered, and biotechnologists started to experiment with it.

Cutting and pasting

If the 1950s and 1960s were the decades in which scientists unravelled the basics of how genetic information is stored, multiplied and passed on from generation to generation, the 1970s and 1980s formed the period when they started harnessing techniques to move genes from one organism to another. It was the discovery of so-called 'restriction enzymes' that provided scientists with a magnificent tool. Existing in many micro-organisms, these enzymes function like genetic scissors by cutting specific gene sequences out of their surrounding DNA. Several hundreds of such enzymes have already been identified. When transferring the genetic material to a new host, the pasting work is done by another set of enzymes. By the end of the 1970s, the first commercial biotech drug produced by these cutting and pasting techniques was available. The human gene for insulin had been inserted into a bacterium and the product 'Humulin' could then be mass-produced.

Having mastered the transfer of genes to micro-organisms, scientists then turned their attention to more difficult tasks: the genetic engineering of plants. Plant cells are more difficult to handle for several reasons. One is that they can contain many more genes than the relatively simple microbes. Also, unlike bacteria, they have rigid cell walls which are difficult to penetrate. Again, nature itself provided a solution. *Agrobacterium tumefaciens* is a bacterium that naturally infects the genetic system of plants, causing the formation of crown-gall, a common plant tumour. The trick is to remove the tumour-inducing genes from the microbe and replace them with agronomically useful ones. The genetically transformed bacterium is allowed to infect plant cells which then take up the desired genetic trait. In this way scientists already managed to introduce genes coding for insect resistance and herbicide tolerance into several crops.

A limiting factor is that normally, *Agrobacterium* infects only broad-leafed plants, leaving some of the most important cereal crops untouched. But scientists are now studying other vectors, such as viruses, to solve this problem. The most spectacular development is the construction of a 'gene-gun' that blasts genetic particles directly into any host plant. The US transnational company Du Pont, has the exclusive rights, and the gun is advertised as 'easy to use and well within the capabilities of even a small laboratory.'[2] All this might sound like rather straightforward practice, but the reality is far from that. Using microbes or guns to insert a gene into specific crops is the easy part, but the real question is actually to make them work. Gene expression is still little understood. Why do genes in leaves actively promote the production of huge amounts of chlorophyll while the same genes present in roots do not?

Tremendous barriers are also faced in the genetic engineering of animals. Scientists have the opportunity to change the genetic structure of the animal at the beginning of its life – the fertilized egg or embryo. In 1982, scientists successfully transferred a gene from a rat into a mouse. The gene in question coded for a growth hormone, and when incorporated into the little rodent, it resulted in the 'mighty mouse' that reached the cover of the scientific journal *Nature*. The technique involved micro-injection of the genetic material into the mouse's pre-embryo, using a very thin needle. British scientists used another technique by introducing embryonic cells of a goat into the embryo of a sheep. The resulting 'geep' is made up of a mosaic of cells, some carrying the genes from one parent, and some from the other. Other techniques in animal genetic engineering use viruses or electric shocks to drive foreign DNA into animal embryos.

In practice, embryo transfer is more important than genetic engineering, at least at present. For example, the transfer of embryos from high quality cattle into lower-yielding ones is already standard practice in many countries. The advantage is obvious. In 1983 a herd of 500 pedigree Friesian cows left the UK for Egypt in four sealed flasks no bigger than suitcases. The frozen seven-day-old embryos were to be re-implanted into Egyptian cows. Where normally several ships would be needed to transport the cows, the embryos fitted on an airplane seat. Also, by inducing 'super-ovulation' in the mother cow, scientists can yield several dozens of embryos per year from a single cow that would normally produce only one. While the benefits seem spectacular, the dangers are profound as well. A future world covered with uniform, vulnerable and high-yielding Friesians – having replaced indigenous breeds in many parts of the world – is a frightening prospect indeed.

A form of genetic engineering, but normally considered as a different technology, is cell or protoplast fusion. The idea is that by mixing the cell content of different species, which normally would not cross, one can combine the genetic material. This is especially important in the medical field, where scientists have succeeded in fusing cancer cells with cells that produce antibodies that attack unwanted infectious agents. The two together form a handy combination: the cancer cell divides endlessly while the other cell produces the desired substances – monoclonal antibodies. Cell fusion is also being worked on in plants and though no major commercial results have yet materialized, the prospects are highly interesting as it offers the possibility of bringing together crop varieties with distant relatives, thus broadening available genetic variation.

About language and limitations

The US biotechnology company Genex, in its 1982 annual report, used an interesting analogy to explain what genetic engineering is all about:

> DNA can be thought of as a language, the language in which all nature's genetic information is written. As with any language, it is desirable to be able to read, write and edit the language of DNA. Rapid methods for determining the substructure of DNA, developed a half a dozen years ago, correspond to reading DNA. These methods now make it possible to determine the complete structure of a gene in a few weeks. New and still rapidly evolving methodologies for chemical synthesis of DNA molecules make it possible to write in the language of DNA much more rapidly than was possible only a couple of years ago. Finally, and most important, genetic engineering techniques themselves make it possible to edit the language of DNA. It is by this editing process that the naturally occurring text can be rearranged for the benefit of the experimenter.[3]

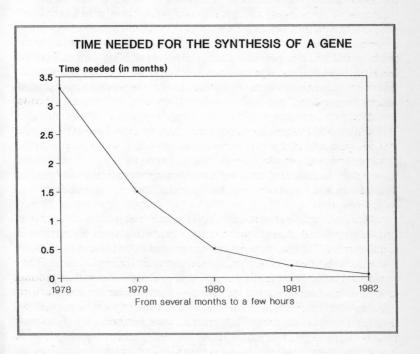

TIME NEEDED FOR THE SYNTHESIS OF A GENE

From several months to a few hours

The biotechnologist as a desk-top publisher – the comparison is an intriguing one. As electronic desk-top publishing made giant leaps forward when computers and software became available, the cutting and pasting of the hereditary material became possible with molecular techniques to read and gene-machines to write DNA sequences. Graph 3.1 shows how fast the technology has developed. In the late 1970s, the synthesizing of a simple gene could take several months, a process which, through automation, is being rapidly standardized. But the desk-top publishing analogy also serves to show the tremendous difficulties still faced by genetic engineers. Ever sat in front of a computer, staring at the message 'disk error, please exit!', thus losing several hours of work? The average word-processor user, like myself, has little understanding of exactly how a computer and its software do its work. You type letters on the keyboard and they appear on the screen. The level of understanding that the biotechnologist has of living organisms is similar. Genetic material can be read, written and edited, but the understanding of how and why genes express themselves, how they really function in a living being and what is their precise role in the overall picture, is largely a mystery.

In part the question is simply to refine the technology, further to deepen the understanding of genetics. But the problem also lies with the limited focus of molecular biology itself. A quote from Edward Yoxens's excellent though by now somewhat outdated book, *The Gene Business*, might be appropriate:

> For molecular biologists, life is what genes do. For them genes are the key to life, and one need look no further than this for the central problems of biology. In their hands biology has become a kind of flatland in which the only activity is the processing and transmission of genetic information . . . I prefer to think of molecular biology as the expression of a Meccano view of nature. With a fairly simple conceptual kit and with a limited number of elements, molecular biologists have been able to represent living nature with a series of increasingly complex mechanical models. They have spent years figuring out what pieces there are in nature's Meccano set, and how they fit together. Some of the more theoretically inclined have examined the very principles of construction, the rules of order and geometry built into the Meccano parts. And now, finally, since the early 1970s they have figured out how to start bolting pieces together, making new models that are not even in the instruction books.[4]

While discussing biotechnology it is tempting to focus predominantly on genetic engineering – recombinant DNA technology – as being the most challenging and dramatic. It is, however, important to stress that recombinant DNA technology is only one of the instruments in the biotechnology tool kit. Biotechnology is a very broad term, for which many different definitions have been given. One widely used description of biotechnology includes 'any technique that uses living organisms (or parts of organisms) to make or modify products, to improve plants and animals, or to develop micro-organisms for specific uses'.[5] This, indeed, includes the whole spectrum of new and old biotechnologies from simple plant-breeding to high-tech gene transfer. Generally referred to as the new biotechnologies, are the basic techniques that have been developed and/or perfected in the past two or three decades. Apart from recombinant DNA techniques, they include tissue culture, cell fusion, enzyme and fermentation technology and embryo transfer. None of them make much sense on their own. It is the *integrated* use of all these different technologies that make the new biotechnologies so powerful and commercially interesting.

Table 3.1
Milestones in biotechnology

7000 BC	Sumerians brew beer.
4000 BC	Egyptians leaven bread with yeast.
1860s	Mendel postulates laws of inheritance. Pasteur discovers that fermentations are performed by micro-organisms
1878	First pure bacterial culture
1900	Hugh de Vries 'rediscovers' Mendel's theories
1920s	Microbial protein produced in continuous fermentation
1939	Plant cells grown in suspension for the first time
1939–45	Commercial process of penicillin production
1944	Oswald Avery recognizes DNA as carrying hereditary factors
1953	Watson and Crick reveal three-dimensional structure of DNA as 'double helix'
1950s	Later in the decade first plants from tissue culture regenerated
1962	First 'codon' of a gene deciphered
1966	Entire genetic code of DNA deciphered
1970	Restriction enzymes used to cut DNA
1973	First gene transfer with rDNA technique from one bacterium into another
1976	Genentech, first company to commercialize rDNA technology founded
1981	First transgenic animal (mouse)
1983	Gene transfer and expression from bacterium to plant, and from plant to plant
1989	PGS announces the cloning of a male sterility gene to develop commercial hybrids for all crops
1990	Several companies announce success with 'gene-gun' to engineer any crop genetically

Compiled by author from different sources

Culturing cells and tissues

In crop biotechnology, tissue or cell culture techniques, also referred to as clonal propagation, offer the capacity to isolate tissues and individual cells, and grow them out to whole plants. A tissue culture of no more than one cubic centimetre in size may contain a million virtually identical cells, each carrying the potential to become an entire new plant. The technique involves the exposure of the tissue or cell to a cocktail of nutrients and hormones that encourage the development of undifferentiated plant tissue. Once formed, other hormones are added to encourage leaves and roots to be formed, after which the plantlet can be potted in soil.

Tissue culture gives the plant breeder a very powerful tool for speeding up breeding work. Using traditional techniques of crossing and back-crossing different varieties, it can take a breeder from seven to 15 years to produce a new variety. In the case of slow-maturing crops, such as trees, the time scale is even longer. Although scientists still face serious problems with regeneration, tissue culture has already reduced the time necessary to develop oil-palm varieties by a factor of 30![6] The same technique also enables the evaluation of germplasm for some characteristics to be performed on a growing mass of cells in a Petri dish rather than having to wait until the actual plant has grown out. Also, it can be used to create new variability since spontaneous mutation commonly occurs during regeneration. Breeders can screen this 'somaclonal variation' for useful traits, giving enormous possibilities for the selection and isolation of new strains with valuable characteristics.

Apart from speeding up and expanding the art of plant breeding, tissue culture also offers the possibility of producing plantlets for direct use in the farmers' fields. Though not yet technically feasible for many crops, commercial success has been achieved with some. This offers new possibilities for mass production, particularly of crops which are normally difficult to multiply. Also, virus free plantlets can be produced and distributed for crops which suffer from diseases in the planting material. Finally, tissue culture can provide an effective new tool for the conservation of germplasm, especially for those plants that propagate vegetatively or for crops that produce seeds that cannot be stored in conventional gene banks. The International Centre for Tropical Agriculture (CIAT) in Colombia holds about 3,000 samples of tissue-cultured cassava varieties *in vitro*. The Internatinal Potato Centre in Peru is doing the same with the potato.[7]

While offering exciting possibilities for crop agriculture, the massive use of tissue culture also has its darker sides. One is that widespread use of tissue-cultured crops will result in a tremendous increase of genetic uniformity, as all offspring are genetically identical. This spells high vulnerability, and a resulting increase in the use of farm chemicals. Also, tissue-cultured plantlets tend to be more expensive for the farmer. In 1983 Unilever's cloned oil-palm plantlets were 18 times more expensive than the normal ones.[8] Finally, the use of tissue culture in germplasm conservation has serious limitations and even dangers, as pointed out by FAO. The same 'somaclonal variation', that provides breeders with new genetic combinations to select from, is a nuisance in conservation as in the end something quite different from the original parent might be conserved.[9]

The regeneration of tissues and individual cells into entire plants is a formidable tool for the plant breeder, but the culturing of plant cells to directly obtain useful products offers even greater possibilities for food and pharmaceutical industries. Many plants are not grown for direct consumption, but for the useful 'secondary metabolites' which they contain. Medicinal plants are one example, but so are the many shrubs and flowers that produce flavours, fragrances and dyestuffs. What would be nicer than having individual plant cells of such crops produce those valuable substances directly, rather than depending on agriculture to grow out the entire plant? People have used cell cultures for many years with yeast when making wine, beer or bread, but those practices are based on naturally occurring microorganisms. Now biotechnology helps to make it feasible with individual cells. While some commercial success has already been achieved for specific high value plant compounds, this is a technology which is just starting to take off. Scientists still face many technical problems and questions of economic efficiency. But the market stakes are enormous and many firms are now focusing their research in this field. As explained later, cells cultured for these purposes can have tremendous economic benefits for the industries involved, while at the same time spelling disaster for the farmers and countries that now grow the crops which may become obsolete.

Closely linked to plant cell-culture techniques is the work on artificial seeds. Several companies and research institutions are working to perfect techniques whereby plant embryos are mass-produced in fermentation tanks, and later encapsulated in a hard gel to mimic the form and functions of a normal seed. A natural seed is the offspring of two parents, the product of fertilization. An artificial seed is the identical copy of one individual, derived from somatic cells. To some extent, artificial seed technology is a sophisticated method of tissue culture. The end product, in this case, is not a cloned plantlet but an encapsulated somatic embryo. This, again, is a technology that is just starting to take off. Currently, it is only worth pursuing for plants with high value seeds, mainly vegetables. It might, however, have enormous implications for agriculture in the long run.

Controlling the process

Enzyme and fermentation technology is so old and widely used that it is often forgotten as one of the crucial elements of the new biotechnologies.

Denominated as 'bioprocess technology' by the US Office of Technology Assessment,[10] it involves the production of desired substances by cells or micro-organisms at an industrial scale. Fermentation has been used by humanity since its very beginning, to preserve food, or simply to make it taste better. In its simplest form it consists of letting microbes go to work on basic food stuff thus transforming its structure or flavour. Perhaps the masters of fermentation technology are the Japanese with their age old experience in the production of soybean sauce and paste, using microbes. With the new biotechnologies the same principles are applied to mass-produce cells, embryos, and any other part of living matter. The system is being made more efficient through the use of specific enzymes that do the same job as the microbes. Often this approach is limited by the problem that the cells and enzymes are mixed with the end-product, which therefore has to be cleaned up afterwards. But now, several techniques for immobilizing both enzymes and cells are being developed to get around that problem.

Among the new biotechnologies, enzyme and fermentation technologies are generally seen as the 'scaling-up' tools to create large quantities of certain products, using cells or enzymes that have been carefully designed by the biotechnologists. Indeed, much of today's cell culture technology would make no commercial sense if at some point the end result could not be scaled-up in fermentation tanks. The same is true for artificial seed technology, and for many other pharmaceutical and food related biotechnologies.

A new threshold?

This brief overview of the tool-box of the new biotechnologist shows one thing very clearly: the potential is enormous. We have focused here on agriculture and food, but the new biotechnologies are being applied in such diverse fields as health care, energy, chemicals, cosmetics and many other areas. Several observers, perhaps in an attempt to tone down the huge expectations but also the genuine concerns, stress that biotechnology as such is nothing new. Indeed, humanity has been transforming living matter since civilization began. Now, however, we are reaching a point where centuries of discoveries are coming together to form a technological blockbuster without precedent. There are three crucial elements in play. First, speed and scale: scientists now carry out complex processes with a routine unimaginable only a few years ago. Tissue culture techniques have dramatically cut the time necessary for breeding new varieties, and improved enzyme and fermentation techniques allow substances to be mass-produced. Secondly, and for the first time in history, nature's reproductive barriers can be torn down and trespassed: human genes are moved into bacteria, plant genes to animals and vice versa. Mice are linked up with rats and sheep with goats. Both fantastic and frightening if you think of all the possible applications. Finally, and perhaps most important, the technology is reaching a stage where lots of money is to be made out of it all.

The estimates of the future market for biotechnology products run into many billions of dollars. Some point to the medical applications already available; others stress the tremendous potential for transforming agriculture and food production. The actual dollar figures put forward by industry analysts vary considerably, with many of them being wild exaggerations, but the general conclusion is clear: the potential of the technology and the commercial markets at stake is enormous, especially for agriculture. There is no doubt that the progress which has been set in motion during the past decades will continue. There is also no doubt that the commercial market will increase. The question is whether the potential of biotechnology to solve some of the most pressing problems of humanity, especially in the Third World, will be realized. To approach this question it is necessary to analyse the development of the technology in its international socio-economic context and to have a closer look at the main actors involved.

Notes and references

1. Quoted in Susan George, *Ill Fares the Land*, Penguin Books, London, 1990, p. 109.

2. Advertisement in *AgBiotechnology News*, March/April 1990, p. 26.

3. Quoted in John Elkington, *The Gene Factory*, Century Publishing, London, 1985, p. 24.

4. Edward Yoxen, *The Gene Business*, Pan Books, London, 1983, pp. 33–5.

5. US Office of Technology Assessment, *Commercial Biotechnology, An International Analysis*, OTA, Washington, 1984, p. 3.

6. Jack Kloppenburg, Martin Kenney: 'Biotechnology, Seeds, and the Restructuring of Agriculture', in *The Insurgent Sociologist*, Vol. 12, No. 3, Cornell University, Ithaca, Summer 1984.

7. FAO, 'Implications of New Biotechnologies for the International Undertaking', Paper for the Commission on PGR, CPGR/89/9, Rome, April 1989, p. 2.

8. John Elkington, 1985, op. cit., p. 112.

9. FAO, 1989, op. cit., p. 3.

10. See OTA, 1984, op. cit., pp. 44–57.

4. The Actors

'We biotechnologists got our message out to the world about fifteen years ago and we said, "There is a revolution coming."'
(P.S. Carlson of Crop Genetics Int'l, 1988)[1]

'The trouble with revolutions is that they get in the hands of the wrong people.'
(Raymond Chandler, novelist, 1943)[2]

'The dream is dead.' In these four words *The Economist* summarized a feeling that many observers of the biotech industry had when the Swiss Pharmaceutical giant Hoffmann-La Roche took over biotechnology's shining star: Genentech.[3] The dream was about entrepreneurial success in biotechnology: university professors with sharp brains and commercial minds setting up small biotech companies that could grow into multimillion dollar empires. The parallel with the computer industry, where such companies as Apple, starting from scratch, are now challenging IBM and others, was often drawn. The dream was also about a highly diverse biotechnology sector with hundreds of independent small biotechnology companies competing shoulder to shoulder with large transnational corporations, thus guaranteeing a highly dynamic interaction responding to the real needs of the marketplace.

If any company stood a chance in following the 'Apple example', it was San Francisco's Genentech. Founded as one of the first 'biotech start-up' companies in 1976, it has, indeed, been a rising star. Putting biotechnology to use in human health care, the company seemed well on its way to making the dream come true: total sales went up from $90 million to $400 million between 1985 and 1989, while net profits grew from $5.6 million to $44 million over the same period.[4] Among the 'new biotechnology firms' (NBFs) it became unquestionably the most successful. While most of the other NBFs are deep in the red as promising R&D does not automatically translate to marketable products, Genentech already had two genetically engineered 'blockbuster' drugs (t-PA and hGH) on the market bringing in $318 million in 1989.[5] Even those analysts who predicted a total shake-out in the biotech industry, usually pointed to Genentech as one of the few companies likely to make it on its own feet.

That was not to be. The bid of Hoffmann-La Roche amounted to a staggering $2.1 billion for 60% of the company's shares, an offer that could not be refused. Additionally, this sturdy pharmaceutical giant from Switzerland has the right to buy the remaining 40% at an already agreed price. Many industry representatives expect that the Genentech buy-out will trigger-off a whole series of further acquisitions of the NBFs working on genetically engineered health-care products. In fact, in terms of who controls the research, the question of whether such an acquisition wave will materialize or not is of limited importance. The terms of the research for both subsidiaries and NBFs are set mostly by the multinationals. This is why *The Economist* describes NBFs as 'research boutiques working on behalf of traditional pharmaceutical companies.'[6]

Public or private?

The history of commercial biotechnology is a short one. The history of its transfer from the public to the private domain is likely to be extremely short as well. As with most other new technologies, biotechnology was born in the laboratories of universities and other public research institutions. Before anyone even knew the word, scientists were there, uncovering step by step the secrets of nature and moving steadily ahead in the fields of molecular biology, biochemistry and genetics. Commercial interest grew only when the integration of all these different research areas seemed to offer interesting marketing opportunities. It started on a small scale. University professors built their own small companies on campus, drawing heavily from university research; this was especially the case in the United States. But although small biotechnology companies that started up during the past decade still gain most of the publicity, it is now the giant agro-chemical, pharmaceutical and food-processing transnationals that dominate the research and the markets. Susan George perhaps described this process best when writing:

> Today's biotechnology came from the work of thousands of people who patiently dug the foundations, built the walls and raised the roofbeams of an enormous edifice. These prodigious labours now accomplished, corporations new and old are jostling one another on the building site to put the final slates on the roof and call the whole place their own.[7]

Some TNCs had already begun to invest in biotechnology at the end of the 1970s, but most of them did not become active in this field until the early 1980s. Despite their brief involvement they already exert substantial control on biotechnology research. According to a report for the World Bank, total R&D in biotechnology worldwide amounted to some $4 billion annually in 1985.[8] *Businessweek* put the figure for 1990 at some $11 billion.[9] The same report calculates that roughly two-thirds of biotech spending comes from the private sector. Industry sources put this figure closer to three-quarters.[10] But even these figures tend to underestimate the dominant role of the private sector. Much of the public spending consists of direct governmental grants to the private sector. West Germany's Science and Technology Ministry hands out project grants to industry of up to 40% of total project costs, while the Dutch Ministry of Economic Affairs provides for grants up to 45% for corporate research programmes 'to help industries direct their national research efforts to new areas of biotechnology.'[11] The UK Government directly co-sponsored the establishment of two biotech companies, Celltech Ltd (1980) and Agricultural Genetics Company (1983). Most other industrialized countries also hand out grants to stimulate corporate-public linked research projects where, again, the corporations profit from the tax payer's money.

Perhaps the boldest 'public spending' initiatives on biotechnology come from the European Commission, where through a whole series of different programmes public money is channelled into the private sector. Fancy names such as BAP, BRIDGE, ECLAIR and FLAIR all stand for massive funding mechanisms on biotech-related research in which industry is heavily involved. Between 1985 and 1994, the European Commission will have spent some $340 million on these projects alone.[12] The giant EEC 'Eureka' project, initiated in 1985 and aiming to promote the European technological R&D base, had, by the end of 1989, handed out over $6 billion, of which almost half a billion was for biotech research.[13] The project aims to spend over $1.2 billion on biotech research in this decade. Most of the grants are for projects in which industry participates. Those who benefit most are Europe's largest agro-chemical, seed and food-processing companies. The situation in the United States is hardly any different. According to the Organization for Economic Co-operation and Development (OECD), US public funding for biotechnology was some $600 million in 1986.[14] The OECD does not tell us how much of this public spending ends up in private companies, but the American case is likely to be similar to Europe's.

Dominance of transnational corporations (TNCs)

Just two US chemical companies, Monsanto and Du Pont, have together an annual biotech-related R&D budget of some $390 million.[15] Other chemical giants such as Eli Lilly, Schering-Plough and Hoffmann-La Roche each spent an annual $60 million on biotech as early as 1982,[16] a figure that has at least doubled since then. TNCs with comfortable turnover figures that run into several or many billions of dollars can support these mega-investments without a dire need for short-term returns in the field of biotechnology. By comparison, a typical NBF spends an annual $5–10 million or so on R&D, much of it contracted by a TNC, while running substantial losses on the whole operation.

The Japanese started late, but are catching up fast. Virtually all corporate biotech research in Japan is done by giant chemical and pharmaceutical companies, together spending $1.4 billion on biotech in 1989 alone, while the government handed out another $550 million, much of which went into co-operative projects with the industry.[17] The big biotech names in Japan include Mitsubishi (Number One in chemicals), Ajinomoto (the largest food-processor), Kirin Brewery (the biggest brewery) and Kyowa Hokko Kogyo (big in chemicals), each of them annually spending between $60 million and $75 million on biotech R&D.[18] 'The Japanese obviously have a lot of money,' remarks industry analyst Robert Kupor. 'They have targeted biotech as a major area they would like to get into.'[19] Apart from increasing in-house research, the Japanese giants are now actively shopping around in the US and Europe for qualified biotech expertise. They find much of it in NBFs, several of which have already accepted substantial equity investments from their big Japanese brothers.

When looking at the structure of the biotechnology industry in the North, some geographical distinctions have to be made. In Japan, biotechnology is almost exclusively developed in the laboratories of the large TNCs. In the United States, most of the money spent on biotech also comes from TNCs, with a myriad of smaller NBFs puttering along to survive in market niches or offering their skills to their larger brothers through contract research. Most of these NBFs are the biotech 'research boutiques', referred to earlier. In Europe, it depends where you are. In France, Germany and Switzerland, there is hardly any opportunity for small venture capital biotech companies, and research is mainly in the hands of the traditional drug and chemical giants. The UK offers a picture similar to that in the USA, as several NBFs were formed and are trying to survive like their counterparts across the Atlantic.

Some industry analysts point to the fact that new NBFs are still being set up, thus promising a growing diversification of the sector. But a closer look at the founders of these new companies reveals that many of them are being set up as joint ventures by TNCs which are already dominating the sector. Of the 135 NBFs founded in 1988–89, as listed in the French biotech magazine *Biofutur*, most have been set up or are controlled by the larger corporate groups. Some of them, focusing on agricultural biotechnology, are listed in Table 4.1. These are the 'true' New Biotechnology Firms. Born out of the need of TNCs to pool their expertise together, they are controlled, financed and run by the true masters of the bio-revolution.

In the turmoil of TNCs throwing their weight behind the biotech boom, the original NBFs have a hard time surviving. Some industry executives expect that nearly half of all US NBFs will be taken over within a decade, and a third of them within the next five years.[20] This might even happen more quickly in the ag-biotech sector, where commercial products still have to find their way to the market. Faced with huge R&D costs and meagre sales, the original NBFs have three options for survival. One is to do contract research for TNCs, on which virtually all of them are eking out their living. The second is to try to stay in the race by merging with other NBFs. Finally, there is the increasingly prevalent move to sell out to the TNCs.

Of the typical ten major NBFs working on agriculture in 1985, few were left in their original position in 1990. Internal cannibalism has raged among the NBFs in recent years. DNAP took AGS, Biotechnica swallowed up the ag-biotech division of Molecular Genetics, and Calgene bought Plant Genetics. As well, external investment has been pouring in from the big groups. Japan Tobacco bought 25% of Belgium's PGS, of which Sandoz already controlled ten per cent. With the take-over of Hilleshög, Sandoz also obtained 15% of AGS. Du Pont bought 15 million shares of DNAP. The list goes on. Finally, straightforward take-overs by TNCs have transfigured the NBF panorama as Lubrizol took full control of Sungene and British American Tobacco Co. took over the ag-biotech research centre of Twyford. Table 4.2 lists some of the latest investment manoeuvres.

If all these names and abbreviations make you dizzy, just take a look at Table 4.3, where the R&D expenses of the top 25 agricultural biotechnology companies according to two investment-analysing houses are listed. Only four of the original NBFs managed to get on the list: DNAP, Calgene, PGS and Agricultural Genetics. The vast majority are TNCs and their subsidiaries. Yet this is still a distorted picture, biased towards the smaller companies. Firstly, the US and European investment analysts do not include the Japanese situation, where TNCs dominate the scene. Secondly, the NBFs listed are to a large extent already controlled by the TNCs in the same table either through equity investment or through contract research. Finally, the TNC figures are grave underestimates, as only agricultural biotech spending is listed. Many TNCs have total annual biotechnology R&D expenses of $100 million and more, only a part of which is dedicated specifically to agriculture. It is precisely the integration of different sectors (medicine, food, pesticides, seeds) which forms the formidable strength of biotechnology for companies which are involved in several fields. A major breakthrough in, for example, tissue culture research might be of use for different parts of the same TNC. The seeds division might use it in improving new plant varieties, the pesticide division could find it helpful for developing their products, and for the pharmaceutical researchers it might provide a powerful tool to screen potential medicinal plants for useful

Table 4.1
The 'true' new biotechnology firms

NBF	Activity	Founder	Comment
Agrisense	AgBiotech	Provesta and Dow Corning	Joint venture of the two corporations
Beghin Meiji	Sweeteners	Beghin-Say and Meiji Seika Kaisah	
Biocode Ltd.	DiagKits	Shell	Full subsidiary
Bionks Co.	AgBiotech	Kyowa Hakko Kogyo and NPI	Joint venture, Sumitomo Corp. also involved
Chembred	AgBiotech	American Cyanamid	Fully owned
Clause Genetic System	AgBiotech	Clause and PGS	50:50 joint venture
Danisco	AgBiotech	DD-Sukker, DD-Sprit and Danisco	Fusion of the three companies, $1.8 billion estim. turnover
DiaPlus	DiagKits	Hoffm.-La Roche and NPA Biotechnologia	Joint venture of the Swiss TNC and USSR company
FloriGene	AgBiotech	Sandoz, DNAP and others	Sandoz involved via Zaadunie
Fresh World	AgBiotech	Du Pont and DNAP	Joint venture
Gene Shears PTY	AgBiotech	Limagrain and CSIRO	$20 million investment by Limagrain in this Australian project
Grand Biotech. Co.	AgBiotech	Miyoshi, Tokyo Menka Kaisha and KYS	Joint venture of the two Japanese companies and a seed company from Taiwan
Huale Seeds	AgBiotech	Sapporo Breweries & National Seed Corp.	Joint venture of Japanese and Chinese groups
Keygene	AgBiotech	Rabo-Biotech Venture Fund	Rabo is large bank in the Netherlands
Mecor Inc.	BioFood	Meiji Seika Kaisha	Fully owned by the Japanese TNC
Micro-Bio Rhizogen	AgBiotech	AGC and RhizoGen Corp.	Joint venture
Oxford Glyco-systems	Carbohydr.	Monsanto and others	Also involved: Adven Ltd., Alafi Capital Corp. and Univ. of Oxford

SDS AgroChem Sandoz and Showa Denko	Joint venture of Swiss and
Biotech KK	Japanese groups
Valent AgBiotech Sumitomo and Chevron	New American subsidiary of
USA Corp.	the two TNCs
(USA)	

Source: 'Les Accords de l'Année 1988' and 'Accords 1989', in *Biofutur*, special supplements, 1989 and 1990. Complemented by other published sources.

properties. In that context, it would be more realistic to add a portion of the basic biotech research to the agri-biotech spending, in which case the NBFs would completely disappear from the horizon.

'Interfirms Cooperation Agreements' (ICAs) are another feature of increasing importance in shaping the global biotechnology market of the future. They draw from an industrial strategy whereby companies that have complementary expertise or parallel market interests co-operate on a selective basis with their main competitors. Such contracts between TNCs and the biotech research boutiques have already been mentioned, but increasingly TNCs are slashing deals amongst themselves as well. 'Biotechnology networks' are proliferating like mushrooms in most OECD countries. According to the European Commission, the ultimate goal of such agreements is often the take-over of one partner by the other. But it can also be an effective way of dividing markets and sharing the cost of research in a way that is beneficial to both. The end result is even further concentration. In the words of the EEC Commission,

> The science and technology system directly associated with or organized by global companies is increasingly shaped and controlled by tight-knit networks of alliances, integrations, joint ventures and projects.[21]

Graph 4.1 shows how such agreements are spinning a tight little web amongst biotechnology companies.

The Netherlands provides an example of how the sector is being controlled by a few companies. According to a study done by the KNBTB, one of the largest farmers' unions in the country, a full two-thirds of all corporate biotechnology research in the Netherlands is carried out by only four corporations: Gist-Brocades, AKZO-Parma, Unilever and Duphar.[22] Another group of 12 companies, some of them TNCs as well, command an additional 15%. The remaining 20% is done by start-ups and other companies. The NBFs have a limited share, with many of them being controlled by their larger brothers anyway (see Graph 4.2). Between 1980 and 1988, corporate research in this area grew by 75%, with public research falling behind with only 45% growth in the same period. But control is not only measured by looking at R&D spendings. Much of the so-called public re-

Table 4.2
Investments in food- and agriculture-related biotech companies
(Take-overs and equity investments, 1988–1990, selected cases)

Company	Partner	Activity	Comment
Biotechnica (USA)	Molecular Genetics (USA)	agbiotech	Biotechnica buys MG's germplasm and plant breeding divisions for some $4 million
Biotechnica (USA)	Several	seeds	The agricultural division of the American biotech company bought four US seed companies: McAllister Seed, Horizon Seeds, Plant Science Research, Flanagan Soybean Research Co.
Booker	Daehnfelt (DK)	seeds	Controlling interest acquired in Feb. 1988; planned to bid for remaining shares
British Am. Tobacco	Twyford Int'l (UK)	agbiotech	The TNC buys the UK biotech research centre of Twyford
Calgene (USA)	Desert Cotton Co. (USA)	seeds	Desert Cotton bought by Calgene's subsidiary, Stoneville Pedigree Seed
Calgene (USA)	Plant Genetics Inc. (USA)	agbiotech	Calgene takes over Plant Genetics
Danisco (DK)	Three Danish companies	food/seed	Danske Sukkerfabbrikker, Danske Spritfabbrikker and Danisco fuse into a new company: Danisco. Strong in agricultural biotech, seeds and food processing
DNAP (USA)	AGS (USA)	agbiotech	DNAP buys Advanced Genetic Sciences
ICI (UK)	Contiseed (USA)	seeds	ICI buys Contiseed from Continental Grain for $50 million. Strong in Latin America, Australia and Thailand
Japan Tobacco (J)	Plant Genetic Systems (B)	seeds	Japan Tobacco buys 25% of PGS ($6 million)
Kirin Brewery (J)	Tokita Seed (J)	seeds	Kirin buys 20% of Tokita Seed, currently No. 14 in Japanese seed production
Kubota (J)	Mycogen (USA)	biopestic.	Kubota intends to buy 14% of the US biotech firm Mycogen, specialized in the field of biopesticides
Limagrain (F)	Picard & Co. (UK)	seeds	The French leader in seeds strengthens its position in the UK through this acquisition

Limagrain (F)	Shissler Seed Co. (USA)	seeds	Limagrain buys the seeds division of Shissler
Lubrizol (USA)	Sungene (USA)	agbiotech	The TNC, already big in seeds, buys Sungene
Mitsubishi/ Meji (J)	Bio-Isolates (UK)	food	The two Japanese firms bought 22% of BI's capital (for $3.7 million), and obtained exclusive rights to market BI's products in Japan
Mitsubishi (J)	Nestlé (CH)	food	The Japanese TNC buys two companies from Nestlé: Trex (fats) and Princes (canned food). This is considered the first move to strengthen its food and biotech operations in Europe
Procter & Gamble (USA)	Calgene (USA)	agbiotech	P & G buys over 700,000 common shares of Calgene for $5 million
Rhône-Poulenc & Orsan (F)	Clause (F)	seeds	Orsan (daughter of Lafarge-Coppée) and Rhône-Poulenc buy 45% of Clause seed company. Lafarge already had 10%, and the two TNCs have now majority control. All seeds interests were put together in one new company: Aritrois, 50:50 owned by the two TNCs
Rhône-Poulenc (F)	Nordica Int'l Inc. (USA)	food	R-Poulenc buys Nordica, a US company specialized in milk and cheese
Sandoz (CH)	Coker's Pedigree Seed (USA)	seeds	Sandoz's US subsidiary Northrup King buys Cocker's Pedigree Seed Co.
Sandoz (CH)	Hilleshög (S)	seeds	Sandoz buys Hilleshog from Volvo. Buyout includes 10% equity in PGS (Belgium) and 15% in Advance Genetic Science (USA)
Sanofi (F)	King Group (CDN)	Seeds	Sanofi is full daughter of Elf-Aquitaine (F), already a major seed company with 1988 turnover of US$107 million. With the acquisition of King Group, it further strengthens its seeds interests
(USA)	Biotechnica (USA)	agbiotech	State Farm Life Insurance Co. increases its investment in BioTechnica Int'l with US$23 million and now owns 67% of its shares
Shell (UK/NL)	Maxell Hybrids (USA)	seeds	Shell's subsidiary Nickerson Seed buys Maxell. More recently Shell announced that it intends to sell Nickerson
Unilever (UK/NL)	Barenburg Seeds (NL)	seeds	Unilever buys 60% of the Dutch seed company

Unilever (UK/NL)	Biocom Biochemicals (IRL)	food	Unilever buys 74% of the Irish company specialized in enzymes and food colorants
Unilever (UK/NL)	Distillers Yeast Ltd. (UK)	food	Distillers Company Yeast Ltd. bought from Guinness for 26 million pounds sterling. Important for fermentation technology

Sources: Numerous publications, including: *Biofutur*, *AgBiotechnology News*, *Agrow* and *Bio/Technology*, several issues.

search is strategically oriented by TNCs, either straightforwardly through contract research at the universities, or through a direct voice in the priority-setting process which governs the public research agenda.

The main instrument of the Dutch government in directing public research is the so-called 'IOP-b Programme', a funding mechanism to promote public biotech research, set up in 1981. A survey was held among companies as to what the research priorities should be. In the first survey round, only the eight largest companies were involved. In the second, among 49 small- and medium-size companies, the Dutch commission concluded that since the smaller companies did not oversee the whole field of research, their views should not be taken into account. As a result, the TNCs now heavily control the direction of the whole programme. Of all seats available in the different committees to decide on the spending of the IOP-b budget, over one-third have been assigned to private companies, with over half of these being occupied by the four top TNCs.[23]

TNC control of public research has been subject to intense debate and concern. There is probably no other field of science where corporations have entered the university campus in such a big way. Universities and other public institutions, under pressure from budget cuts and austerity programmes, are looking for additional funding, while TNCs sniff around for cheap labour. The new marriages might be beneficial for both, one could say: the TNC makes the funds available and the university carries out the research. Monsanto 'donated' $23.5 million to Washington University for biotech research; Bayer is contributing to the Max Planck Institute in Cologne for the same purpose; and Hoechst built an entire $70 million biotech research laboratory for the Massachusetts General Hospital where research on crop genetics is also carried out. Lubrizol has more than $20 million tied up in research contracts at 18 universities and other public institutions.[24] These industry-university contracts have caused much controversy for obvious reasons. 'You don't need to know algebra to figure out how that committee works,' says US congressman Albert Gore, talking about the committee that governs the Monsanto/Washington University deal. 'No research can be done unless the company gives permission.'

Table 4.3
Top ag-biotechnology companies' agricultural biotechnology spending in 1988 ($US million)

Company	R&D
1. Monsanto	55
2. Shell*	25
3. Sandoz	17
4. Ciba-Geigy	16
5. DNAP*	15
6. Upjohn	15
7. Enimont*	15
8. Du Pont*	15
9. Rhone-Poulenc	15
10. ICI*	15
11. Elf Aquitaine (Sanofi)*	14
12. Lubrizol (Agrigenetics)*	13
13. Biotechnica*	12
14. Solvay	12
15. Calgene*	11
16. Danisco (DDS)*	9
17. Bayer	8
18. Plant Genetic Systems*	8
19. WR Grace – Cetus (AgraCetus)*	7
20. BASF	7
21. Dekalb-Pfizer*	6
22. Agricultural Genetics*	6
23. Hoechst	5
24. Pioneer Hi-Bred*	5
25. Dow Chemicals*	4
Total Top 25	**330**

* = Plant biotechnology only. The other figures include animal biotechnology as well.

Sources: *AgBiotechnology News*, 'Teweless Ranks Top Seeds, Biotech Firms', July/August 1989, p. 19 (for plant biotech figures, based on study by Teweless & Co.); *Time* magazine, 'High-Chem, special advertising section', 20 November 1989 (based on data from County NatWest WoodMac.). *Agricultural Genetics Report*, 'Multinational Companies Involved in Biotech Seed Research', Vol. 7, No. 5, October 1988.

Burke Zimmerman, then with the biotech company Cetus, says about the Hoechst grant for a biotech laboratory: 'Essentially everyone in that lab is an indentured servant to Hoechst.'[25] In most contracts, the TNC has the right to the first look at the results and can delay publication of them until patent possibilities are investigated. In his excellent study on this matter, Martin Kenney, then professor at Ohio State University, concludes:

THE BIOTECHNOLOGY WEB

COOPERATIVE AGREEMENTS WITHIN THE INDUSTRY

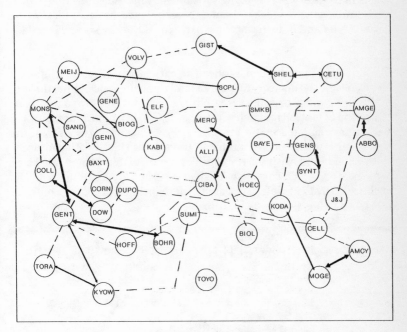

ABBO	Abbot Labs (USA)	GIST	Gist-Brocades (NL)
ALLI	Allied (USA)	HOEC	Hoechst (FRG)
AMCY	American Cyanamid (USA)	HOFF	Hoffmann-La Roche (CH)
AMGE	Amgen (USA)	J&J	Johnson & Johnson (USA)
BAXT	Baxter-Travenol Labs (USA)	KABI	Kabivitrum (S)
BAYE	Bayer (FRG)	KODA	Kodak (USA)
BIOG	BioGen (USA)	KYOW	Kyowa Hakko Kogyo (J)
BIOL	Bio-Logicals (USA)	MEIJ	Meiji Seika Kaisha (J)
BOHR	Bohringer-Ingelheim (FRG)	MERC	Merck (USA)
CELL	Celltech (UK)	MOGE	Molecular Genetics (USA)
CETU	Cetus (USA)	MONS	Monsanto (USA)
CIBA	Ciba-Geigy (CH)	SAND	Sandoz (CH)
COLL	CollaGen (USA)	SCPL	Schering-Plough (USA)
CORN	Corning (USA)	SHEL	Shell (NL/UK)
DOW	Dow Chemical (USA)	SMKB	SmithKline Beckman (USA)
DUPO	Du Pont (USA)	SUMI	Sumitozo Group (J)
ELF	ELF-Aquitaine (F)	SYNT	Syntex (USA)
GENE	Genex (USA)	TORA	Toray (J)
GENI	Genetics Institute (USA)	TOYO	Toyo (J)
GENS	Genetic Systems (USA)	VOLV	Volvo (S)
GENT	GenenTech (USA)		

◄─────► 4 or more co-operative agreements

───────── 3 agreements

─ ─ ─ ─ 2 agreements

SOURCE: The FAST II Programme, Results and Recommendations
Volume 1, Commission of the EC, Brussels 1988, p. 71.

The point is not only that the knowledge being sold was paid for by the public but, even more important, that the university, a peculiar and fragile institution . . . is being subsumed by industry, one of the very institutions with which it should, to some degree, be in conflict. When university and industry become partners, the entire society is endangered . . .[26]

The emerging picture, then, is one of an extremely powerful technology mostly developed and controlled by a few large companies, either directly or through control of public research. The picture also shows a total concentration of biotech research within the OECD. In a report for the World Bank it is calculated that up to 1985 only $300 million (or 7.5% of the global figure) was spent on biotech R&D outside the US/EEC/Japan bloc.[27] With Canada and Australia responsible for most of this amount, the Third World emerges as a complete outsider in the bio-revolution. With the explosive growth in biotech research in the North since 1985, this outsider role is becoming ominously inextricable.

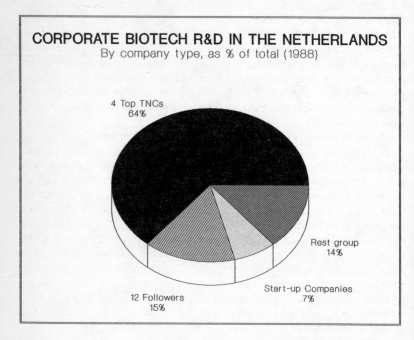

CORPORATE BIOTECH R&D IN THE NETHERLANDS
By company type, as % of total (1988)

4 Top TNCs 64%

Rest group 14%

Start-up Companies 7%

12 Followers 15%

The concentration within

The few are becoming fewer, and the big grow bigger. The pace of the concentration process among the largest agrochemical, seed, drug and food houses is astonishing. The concentration of biotechnology within the hands of TNCs is happening at the same time as an explosive take-over wave amongst the big companies themselves.

The pesticide sector is an example of where this is happening. Where 30 manufacturers were engaged in pesticides development in the mid-1970s in the United States, there are only a dozen today; the situation in Europe is similar.[28] With a global market of some $20 billion, the top ten companies are now controlling a full three-quarters of it. (See Table 4.4.) With few small pesticide companies left to buy up, the take-over mania is now being extended into a fierce fight between the TNCs themselves. In the past few years ICI bought Stauffer Chemicals, Rhône-Poulenc took the pesticides division from Union Carbide, and the two large US chemical groups, Dow Chemical and Eli Lilly, merged their pesticides business into a new company: Dow Elanco.[29] To stay in the race, Hoechst had to buy Celanese, and Du Pont the US Shell pesticides business. Though it may seem that there is no room for further concentration, industry analysts predict that the mergers will continue.[30] Apart from sheer company size, biotechnology is acclaimed as the main factor in determining who will stay in the race for domination of the pesticide market. *All* of the top ten pesticide producers fall in the group of the largest agricultural biotechnology companies listed in Table 4.3. Many of them have substantial plant-breeding operations as well.

If the concentration among the pesticides groups has been dramatic, the shake-out in the pharmaceutical sector is even more spectacular. For decades, the top 30 drug producers have remained the same, although their ranking might have changed. Ten corporations now control some 28% of the world market, as a result of an enormous merger wave in the sector. Table 4.5 shows the global ten pharmaceutical giants, and lists the recent mergers and take-overs. Apart from the Monsanto buy-out of Searle (1985) and the Kodak acquisition of Sterling Drugs, all major take-overs took place in 1989–90, and there are a lot more to come. In total, the drug giants spent over $40 billion in such take-overs in these two years alone. Even after the recent merger-mania no single TNC has more than a four per cent share of the world market. According to Mads Olvilsen, the boss of the Nordic pharmaceutical company Novo, a handful of TNCs are now heading for global market shares of over ten per cent each.[31] Here again, the control over biotechnology seems the deciding factor for the future. While many see the Genentech take-over by Hoffmann-La Roche as only the first step in a major acquisition drive of smaller pharmaceutical biotech companies by TNCs, others think it will depend more on the extent that biotech re-

Table 4.4
Top ten pesticide houses
(1988 sales, US$ billion, adapted for recent take-overs)

		Pesticide Sales	% of Global Market
1.	Ciba-Geigy (CH)	2.14	10.70
2.	Bayer (FRG)	2.07	10.37
3.	ICI (UK)	1.96	9.80
4.	Rhone-Poulenc (F)	1.63	8.17
5.	Du Pont (USA)	1.44	7.19
6.	Dow Elanco (USA)*	1.42	7.11
7.	Monsanto (USA)	1.38	6.89
8.	Hoechst (FRG)	1.02	5.12
9.	BASF (FRG)	1.00	5.00
10.	Shell (NL/UK)	0.94	4.69
	Total top ten	**5.00**	**75.02**
	Global Sales	20.00	100.00

* The pesticides divisions of Dow Chemicals and Eli Lilly (Elanco) merged into Dow Elanco in 1989. Other major pesticide companies include (with 1988 pest. sales): Schering ($US0.75 billion), American Cyanamid (USA, $US0.69 billion), Sandoz (CH $US0.60 billion) and Kumiai (J, $US0.46 billion).

Source: *AGROW*, 'Ciba Geigy still number one in 1988', No. 92, 28 July 1989, p. 1.

Table 4.5
The top ten pharmaceutical corporations
(1987 sales in US$ billion, adapted for recent take-overs)

	Pharma. Sales	% of Global Market
Merck (US)	4.23	3.53
SmithKline-Beecham (US/UK)	4.00	3.33
Bristol M.-Squibb (US)	3.90	3.25
Hoechst (FRG)	3.51	2.93
Glaxo (UK)	3.37	2.81
R. Poulenc-Rorer (F/US)	3.30	2.75
Ciba-Geigy (CH)	3.17	2.64
Bayer (FRG)	2.96	2.47
Am. Home Products (US)	2.93	2.44
Sandoz (CH)	2.75	2.29
Total top ten	**34.12**	**28.43**
Global Market	**120.00**	**100.00**

The urge to merge
Mergers and take-overs in the drug industry since 1985

	Combined Sales (est.)	Take-over Cost (est.)
SmithKline - Beecham	5.4	7.9
Bristol Meyers - Squibb	4.1	12.0
American Home Prod. - Robins	3.1	3.2
Dow - Marion	1.9	5.1
Monsanto - GD Searle	1.0	2.1
Eastman Kodak - Sterling	0.8	5.1
Novo - Nordisk	0.6	N.A.
Merieux - Connaught	0.5	N.A.
Rhone Poulenc - Rorer	3.0	1.7
Hoffmann-La Roche - Genentech	N.A.	2.1

Sources: 'Drug Company Mergers', in *The Economist*, 5 August 1989; 'The New World of Drugs', in *The Economist*, 4 February 1989; 'Failed Transactions Marked the Year of Mergers', in *Wall Street Journal (Europe)*, 5 January 1990; 'Biotech Goes Global', in *Business Week*, 26 February 1990.

search will be built-up in-house. Most TNCs follow both strategies.

Yet even before anyone thought of biotechnology as the driving force behind the restructuring of agriculture, TNCs started massively buying up independent seed companies. With or without biotechnology, the seed is the ultimate vehicle of genetic improvements in agriculture, and the TNCs realized the importance of that. Once a highly diverse and often family-based sector with no TNC involvement, virtually all top seed houses now have their main interest in either chemicals, pesticides or pharmaceuticals (Table 4.6). Pioneer Hi-Bred and Limagrain, both primarily seed companies, are the only exceptions. Together the top ten now control over 20% of the global market – a figure that is increasing. ICI, Britain's number one chemical company, for example, aims to continue its spectacular growth in seeds. Entering in the seeds business only in 1985 with its acquisition of Garst Seed (USA), it continued to buy up seed companies in Europe and now has annual seed sales of some $250 million. The firm's objective is to triple this figure before the turn of the century.[32] Another newcomer on the scene is Unilever. Apart from some work on its plantation crops, it had little seed interests until it bought up the Cambridge-based Plant Breeding Institute from the UK Government. After its latest acquisition of Barenburg Seeds in the Netherlands, it now ranks as thirteenth among the world's largest seed companies with annual sales of $110 million.[33] Both companies are heavily committed to biotechnology, with ICI spending half of its R&D budget on it.[34] According to US seed industry consultant William Teweless, the restructuring of the seeds sector is only half completed. He expects that by the year 2000 between ten and 20 TNCs will dominate the entire market.[35]

Table 4.6
Top ten seed corporations
(1988 sales, $US million, adapted for recent take-overs)

		Seed Sales	% of Global
1.	Pioneer Hi-Bred (US)	735	4.90
2.	Sandoz (CH)*	507	3.38
3.	Limagrain (F)	370	2.46
4.	Upjohn (USA)	280	1.87
5.	Aritrois (F)*	257	1.71
6.	ICI (UK)	250	1.67
7.	Cargill (USA)	230	1.53
8.	Shell (NL/UK)	200	1.33
9.	Dekalb-Pfizer (USA)	174	1.16
10.	Ciba-Geigy (CH)	150	1.00
	Total top ten	**3098**	**20.65**
	Global	15000	100.00

* Sandoz bought Hilleshog from Volvo (S), thus substantially increasing its seed sales (up from an estimated $US290 million in 1987). Aritois is a new joint venture in which Rhone Poulenc and Lafarge-Coppee are bringing their seeds interests together. The new group includes Clause, the French market leader in vegetable and ornamental seeds. One study puts seeds sales of Ciba-Geigy as high as $245 million and Aritois sales as low as $104 million. Shell sold off part of its seed interests to Limagrain, thus adding some $100 million to the French company's revenues. Other recent take-overs: Limagrain bought Shissler Seed Co. (USA), ICI bought Contiseed from Continental Grain (USA), Cargill bought Canola Corp., Unilever bought PBI (UK) and Barenburg (NL). Other major seed companies include: KWS (FRG), Lubrizol (USA), Takii (J), Cebeco (NL), Elf Aquitaine (Sanofi - F).

Sources: 'Les chimistes tentent de se constituer de nouveaux bastions sur le marché mondial des semences', in *Le Monde*, Paris, 21 November 1989 (based on ICI estimates); 'Rhone-Poulenc/Lafarge-Coppee seed joint venture', *AGROW*, Richmond UK, No. 95, 8 September 1989; several other issues of *AGROW* were used.

The fourth, and probably in the long-run most dominant, actors in biotechnology are the food processors. 'The greatest impact on food industry costs and profits may stem from research and development in the field of biotechnology.' This was the conclusion of an OECD study on the impact of technology on the food processing industry.[36] Indeed, the food transformers are probably in the best position to reap the benefits of the bio-revolution. The cost of their raw materials is much more of a determining factor than in the other sectors, representing up to two-thirds of the sales value of the food processors.[37] This is exactly where biotechnology can make the difference. With improved enzyme and fermentation techniques, tissue culture and genetic engineering, raw material requirements can be diversified, reduced or eliminated altogether. The same techniques can produce higher yields of crops and animals. They can also modify the components to suit the needs of the industry better. Finally, energy costs can be greatly reduced as the food industries switch from chemical to biological technologies. Higher yields and increased interchangeability tend further to decrease the prices of what is the end product of the farmer but the raw material for the food processor. Chapter 6 explains some of the implications.

One reason why neither the farmers nor the consumers will profit much from all these cost savings is that the industry structure is highly oligopolistic, as shown in the above quoted OECD study. In the USA the four firms accounted for some 45% of the sales, while in the UK the five largest food TNCs commanded up to 70% of the market in the early 1980s.[38] Since then, the major food processors have been involved in a life-and-death acquisition battle involving billions of dollars. Since 1982, a quarter of the 100 largest processors have disappeared into the hungry mouths of even bigger competitors.[39] In 1985 four mergers, together costing over $16 billion, completely changed the US industry: Reynolds took Nabisco (forming RJR Nabisco); Philip Morris took General Foods; Nestlé took Carnation; and Beatrice took Essmark.[40] Later Kraft and RJR Nabisco – both in the top ten listing – were themselves taken-over for $37.5 billion in total. Kraft now belongs to Philip Morris, which thus overtook Nestlé as the number one food processor. RJR Nabisco was taken-over by the US buy-out specialist Kohlberg Kravis Roberts (KKR). Several others followed. Table 4.7 gives a rough approximation of the provisional result up to 1990: the global top ten companies together selling for more than $100 billion a year. 'The food companies haven't finished eating', announces *Business Week*, with industry experts predicting that Europe's 45 major food processors may further merge into ten giant companies within the next few years.[41]

Everybody is trying to fit biotech into its operations: General Foods uses it to produce a caffeine-free coffee bean; Hershey tries to get more cocoa from the cocoa tree or from other crops; Campbell Soups makes high-solid tomatoes; ICI developed an enzyme to speed up cheese ageing; Nestlé modifies soybeans; and Unilever works on everything from cloning plants to producing biotech sweeteners. Either in-house or by contracting NBFs, the food processors are trying to make up for their late entry into the sector. Backed by multi-billion sales, they do not hesitate to put money on the table. Sir Geoffrey Allan puts it this way: 'I could make a small fortune on biotechnology if only I had a larger one to invest in it.'[42] This might be a reason why he is now director of Unilever's Research and Engineering Division. He claims that his company is spending an annual $33 million on applied biotechnology, but other sources calculate the firm's total biotechnology budget to be well over $100 million.[43] Unilever's activities in this field are almost as broad as the company itself: enzymatic modification of fats and gums; new enzymes for detergents; genetic engineering of microbes; genetically engineered sweeteners; tissue culture of plants; pregnancy and ovulation testing kits and so on.

Table 4.7
The top ten food processing corporations (US$ billion)

		Food Sales
1.	Philip Morris (USA)*	20.49
2.	Nestle (CH)*	16.80
3.	Unilever (NL/UK)*	12.45
4.	K.K.R. (RJR Nabisco) (USA)*	10.11
5.	Anheuser-Bush (US)	7.45
6.	Coca-Cola (USA)	7.30
7.	Pepsico (USA)	6.61
8.	Con-Agra (USA)	6.60
9.	S & W Barisford (UK)	6.31
10.	Grand Metropolitan (UK)*	6.04
Total		**100.16**

* In 1989 Kohlberg Kravis Roberts & Co. (KKR) bought RJR Nabisco for $US24.5 billion (RJR Nabisco itself was the result of the acquisition of Nabisco by R. J. Reynolds in 1986). Kraft (previously the No. 5 food processor) was bought up for $US13 billion by Philip Morris, which then overtook Nestle as the world biggest food processor. Nestle took Rowntree (UK) for $US4.6 billion. Unilever bought Cheeseborough-Ponds as well as Brooke Bond. Grand Metropolitan took Pillsbury Co. ($5.7 billion). BSN (F) spent $US750 million in buying 14 food companies in 1988/1989 alone, and reserves $1 billion for additional take-overs.

Sources: Fowler et al., 'The Laws of Life', *Development Dialogue*, 1988, No. 1–2, Dag Hammarsköld Foundation, Uppsala, 1988, pp. 94–8; 'Failed Transactions Marked the Year of Mergers', in *Wall Street Journal (Europe)*, 5 January 1990, p. 23; 'The Food Companies Haven't Finished Eating', in *Business Week*, 9 January, 1989, p. 42.

These companies, then, are the dominating forces in the biotechnology drama. The stage is set after only a decade of commercial biotechnology. Starting in the university laboratories and passing through an exciting but short phase of small, independent biotech companies, the decision on what will happen next lies mostly in the boardrooms of the giant suppliers of agro-chemicals, medicines and processed food. Some directions in these decisions are easy to assess, others more difficult to speculate on. In general, however, boards of directors tend to look at what is best for the company's profit; which is not necessarily the same as the people's well-being. The European Commission tends to agree. In a report on science, technology and the global economy, it comes to the following conclusion:

> The global economy might be increasingly governed by decision making processes and decisions makers primarily reflecting the corporatist, though legitimate, interests of private groups and networks of global firms. In this context, the decision making processes concerning the alloca-

tion of the most important segment of the world human, technical and natural resources will be less and less based on representative democratic procedures.[44]

Notes and references

1. P. S. Carlson, 'One Company's Attempt to Commercialize an Agricultural Biotechnology Technology', in *Strengthening Collaboration in Biotechnology*, Conference Proceedings, AID, Washington, 1989, p. 414.

2. R. Chandler, *The High Window*, Penguin Books, New York, 1943, p. 113.

3. 'Test-tube Trauma: the sale of Genentech', in *The Economist*, Vol. 314, 10 February 1990.

4. UNCTC, *Transnational Corporations in Biotechnology*, UNCTC, New York 1988, p. 36; and 'Test-tube Trauma', op. cit.

5. 'A New Era for Genentech, and So It Goes', in *Bio/Technology*, Vol. 8, No. 3, March 1990, p. 178.

6. 'Test-tube Trauma', op. cit.

7. Susan George, *Ill Fares the Land*, Penguin Books, London, 1990, pp. 115–16.

8. G. Persley, 'Agricultural Biotechnology: Opportunities for International Development', Draft Synthesis Report, World Bank, May 1989, p. 68.

9. 'Japanese Biotech's Overnight Evolution', in *Business Week*, 26 February 1990, pp. 34–6.

10. Keith Pike, Marketing and Sales Director of ICI Seeds, in a letter to Alistair Smith, Surrey (UK), 6 April 1990.

11. OECD, *Biotechnology and the Changing Role of Government*, OECD, Paris, 1988, p. 91.

12. Mark Cantley, 'Managing an Invisible Elephant', in *Biofutur*, No. 84, November 1989, pp. 8–16. Total figure is 280 million ECU.

13. H. Guillaume et al, 'Eureka: Vitesse de Croisière', in *Biofutur*, No. 84, November 1989, pp. 35–6.

14. OECD, 1988, op. cit., p. 92.

15. Jack Doyle, *Altered Harvest*, Viking Press, New York, 1985. Doyle estimates Du Pont's R&D as over $US 200 million and puts the figure for Monsanto at $US 190 million.

16. OTA, 1984, op. cit., p. 74.

17. 'Japanese Biotech's Overnight Evolution', op. cit., pp. 34–6.

18. Ibid., p. 34.

19. Quoted in 'Japanese seem headed toward ownership of US Companies', in *Genetic Engineering News* (GEN), Vol. 10, No. 1, New York, January 1990, p. 36.

20. According to a survey of industry analysts, the Arthur Young Group. Quoted in 'Pendulum is set to swing back', *Financial Times*, 12 May 1989.

21. Commission of the European Communities, *The FAST II Programme, Results and Recommendations*, Vol. 1, Brussels, 1988, p. 69.

22. KNBTB, 'Biotechnologie en Land – en Tuinbouw', The Hague, January 1989.

23. Ibid., p. 24.

24. OTA, 1984, op. cit., pp. 574–7. See also Jack Doyle, 1985, op. cit.; and Martin Kenney, *Biotechnology: The University–Industrial Complex*, Yale University Press, New Haven/London, 1986.

25. Both quotes from Doyle, 1985, op. cit., p. 359.

26. Martin Kenny, 1986, op. cit., p. 246.

27. G. Persley, 1989, op. cit., p. 68.

28. Fowler et al, 'The Laws of Life', in *Development Dialogue*, Dag Hammarskjold Foun-

dation, No. 1/2, 1988, p. 74.

29. Peter Marsh, 'Seeds of Doubt in Agrichemicals', *Financial Times*, 5 May 1989.

30. Allen Woodburn, from the UK stockbroker CNW, quoted in Peter Marsh, 1989, op. cit.

31. 'The New World of Drugs', in *The Economist*, 4 February 1989.

32. 'Seeds, a Natural Route for Biotechnology', in *European Chemical News*, Fertilizers & Agrochemicals Supplement, March 1988. ICI's objective is a seed business of £ Sterling 500 million in the next 15–20 years.

33. 'World Seed Sales Top $15,100 million in 1988', in *AGROW*, No. 102, 15 January 1990, p. 8.

34. 'Seeds a Natural Route . . .', op. cit.

35. Ibid.

36. OECD, 'Technology and the Food Processing Industry', *STI Review*, No. 2. September 1987, OECD, Paris, 1987.

37. Ibid.

. Ibid.

39. Fowler et al, 1988, op. cit., p. 96.

40. OECD, *STI Review*, 1987, op. cit.

41. 'The Food Companies Haven't Finished Eating', in *Business Week*, 9 January 1989, p. 42.

42. Quoted in 'Les Pas de Géant d'Unilever', in *Biofutur*, January 1988, p. 21.

43. J. C. Pinon, 'Financements Nationaux de la R&D en Biotechnologie: Les Années 80', in *Biofutur*, No. 90, May 1990, p. 121. (Figure quoted is 750 million French francs.)

44. Commission of the European Communities, 1988, op. cit., p. 72.

5.   Providing the Inputs

'*In two decades, we won't be spraying crap on plants any more.*'
(Sam Dryden, then President of Agrigenetics, a US biotechnology company)[1]

'*Screening of cultivars for genetic resistance to new, highly potent herbicides, is becoming as important as screening the same cultivars for genetic resistance to prevalent disease and insect pests.*'
(Don Duvick, former director of research of Pioneer Hi-Bred seed company)[2]

Perhaps one of the most exciting and promising possibilities of agricultural biotechnology is to decrease the need for chemical inputs in crop production. Virtually every article on this issue starts off saying that biotechnology has unlimited possibilities in this direction. *Newsweek* promises its readers that biotechnology will produce plants which 'can destroy plant and insect attackers with little or no help from people'.[3] Howard Schneiderman, R&D Director of Monsanto, also paints a bright future:

> I believe . . . that with the new biotechnology almost anything that can be thought of can ultimately be achieved. [He refers specifically to] new treatments for disease, new ways of controlling pests, crops which produce their own pesticides.[4]

This euphoria about the possible impact of biotechnology on agriculture is easy to understand. Biotechnology, at least in theory, can provide the tools for increased pest resistance in crops and for the reduction of dependence on chemical nitrogen fertilizers. Although the work is not as easy as it might seem, it is possible to transfer the genes responsible for pest resistance to crop-plants. Also, research is being carried out to genetically engineer micro-organisms that attack pests and diseases, the so-called biological pesticides.

The breeding of pest resistance into crops has always been a painstaking and expensive job and certainly has not received the attention it deserves. The US Office of Technology Assessment (OTA) believes that in the past decades there was less resistance-breeding because of the availability of cheap pesticides.[5] The main focus of plant-breeding has always been to increase yields rather than to reduce inputs. Private breeding programmes especially lack emphasis on pest-resistance breeding, according to the OTA.[6] In many ways, chemical pesticides were used to compensate for the lack of genetic resistance that might have been bred into crops. Increased emphasis on mono-cropping, based on a few very vulnerable varieties, has served to encourage an agricultural system that needs enormous amounts of pesticides but still loses 20 to 50% of the harvest to pests and diseases.[7] Contrary to the impression generally given, crop losses due to pests and diseases have actually increased during the past 30 years. For example, US farmers lost some seven per cent of their crop to insect pests in the 1940s, a figure that had increased to 13% by 1974.[8]

Will biotechnology reverse this trend toward increased crop vulnerability and associated increased pesticide use? It might and it might not. To a large extent it very much depends on whether research priorities are sufficiently directed towards it. Biotechnology provides some very powerful tools to increase pest resistance in agricultural crops, but it certainly does not automatically cause a major shift to pest-resistance breeding. As pointed out earlier, biotechnology research is heavily dominated by the private industry which might have its own agenda. The OTA clearly had this in mind when it stated that:

> Much of the agricultural research effort is being made by the agricultural chemical industry, and this industry may see the early opportunity of developing pesticide-resistant plants rather than undertaking the longer term effort of developing pest-resistant plants.[9]

In this context, the optimistic expectations of Howard Schneiderman, quoted at the outset of this chapter, should be viewed with some scepticism. Schneiderman's company is among the largest pesticide producers in the world.

The biased focus: herbicide tolerance

Nowhere does the immense discrepancy between potential and actual developments in biotechnology become clearer than with current biotech research on herbicide tolerance. Over the years, the use of herbicides has grown dramatically, as a result of changing agricultural techniques: monocropping, mechanization and non-tillage farming. World sales of herbicides amount to almost $5 billion annually, representing some 40% of total pesticides sales in the world.[10] Although the industry often claims that the newly developed herbicides harm neither humans nor the environment, recent research has detected several cases of carcinogenicity caused by herbicides and toxic herbicide residues in groundwater. In general, very little is known about the long-term effects of herbicide residues in the environment.

One problem that limits the use of herbicides is the fact that many herbicides not only attack the weeds they are supposed to kill, but also harm the crop they are supposed to protect. This restricts the farmer in the amount of herbicide she or he can use. Also, some herbicides might not harm a specific crop, but linger too long in the soil and damage the crop that is planted the next season.

The first efforts to reduce the damage that herbicides can cause to crops, were undertaken by Ciba-Geigy. Ciba, which had already bought up several seed companies in the 1970s, developed a chemical 'coat' for seeds to protect them against the herbicides produced by them. This 'herbishield' was wrapped around Ciba-Geigy seeds, thus providing the company with a double profit: the farmer buys the Ciba-Geigy seeds packaged with the Ciba-Geigy herbicides. After successfully introducing the package in industrialized countries, Ciba is now trying to penetrate the markets of the South.

With biotechnology, this process is being further sophisticated. Millions of dollars are being pumped into research to genetically alter crops in order to resist higher doses of herbicides. In Table 5.1 some of the current research on herbicide tolerance is listed. The main source of this listing is based on 'Derwent Biotechnology Abstracts'.[11] Derwent scans more than 1,000 scientific publications and patents related to biotechnology and provides indexed abstracts each fortnight, thus providing probably one of the most complete sources on biotech research. Added to the listing were the results of a few recent studies on the matter. At least 93 institutions have been involved in research on herbicide tolerance since the mid-1980s. All major crops are subject to the search for tolerance to a whole range of different weed killers. The substantial involvement of universities and other public institutions seems at a first sight surprising (48 public institutions in total). One reason for this might be that public institutions tend to publish more freely, and are thus over-represented in the table.

What the table does not show are the dollar figures attached to the projects. The US based 'Biotechnology Working Group' estimates that publicly funded institutions in the United States alone spent $10.5 million on herbicide tolerance in the past few years.[12] But the major work is done in the corporate laboratories. The public institutions listed in the table generally limit their work to one or two herbicides and only a few crops. Rather than aiming for the commercialization of herbicide tolerant varieties, several of them perform this research to upgrade their knowledge on gene transfer technology in general. In contrast, major pesticide producers such as Monsanto and Du Pont each have a whole range of different projects involving many crops and different chemicals and do focus on the commercialization of the technology. Du Pont alone is investing $13 million in research on tolerance to its new sulfonylurea herbicides.[13] Additionally, most of the work by the smaller biotechnology companies such as Calgene and Plant Genetic Systems is under contract to the TNCs. Keith Pike, Marketing and Sales Director at ICI Seeds, thinks that herbicide tolerance technology is concentrated within a dozen corporations.[14]

No biotechnologically engineered herbicide-tolerant crop has yet reached the farmer's field, but many are now being field tested. The early 1990s are generally seen as the time when the first tolerant crops will become commercially available. If these predictions are confirmed, herbicide tolerance is likely to be the first major result of agricultural biotechnology made available to farmers on a large scale. Opinions differ as to how large. Early estimates talk of an annual value of herbicide-tolerant crops of $2.1 billion by the turn of the century, while other – probably more realistic – projections range from a low $75 million to a high $320 million annually.[15] But apart from the profit from the seeds themselves, the chemical TNCs are also interested in the resulting increased use of the chemicals that are sold with them. Teweless reports that a main reason for being involved in this field is the 'hope of selling the seed and the chemical as a pair' thus creating 'a complementary demand for both chemical and seed'.[16]

A case in point is the work on atrazine, an already widely used herbicide in maize, a crop which is naturally tolerant to it. But soybean, which is often sown in rotation with maize, is very sensitive to the herbicide. As atrazine is persistent and lingers long in the soil, its residues can damage such crops as soybean that are planted the year after. Du Pont has now isolated a gene that enables mutant pigweed to withstand atrazine. According to Charles Arntzen, Du Pont's Associate Director for plant science and microbiology, these mutants 'have a trait that says: "I don't care how much chemical you throw at me, it doesn't faze me" '.[17] Such perspectives don't faze the chemical companies either. Teweless calculates that with the development of atrazine-tolerant soybeans, atrazine sales would increase by about $120 million annually.[18] A study prepared for the European Commission concurs: 'If the predominant varieties of soya bean were resistant to atrazine, about two or three times more atrazine would be used on related crop land.'[19]

Proponents of herbicide tolerance often point out that this would help to eliminate the older persistent and more dangerous class of herbicides in favour of the new and environmentally safe ones. Graph 5.1, which breaks down the data of Table 5.1 by herbicide, shows that this argument does not reflect reality. The old and persistent triazines (including atrazine) are

Table 5.1
Research on herbicide tolerance by private and public institutions

Part 1: Industry

Research by:	Herbicide	Targets
Advanced Genetic Sciences, USA	Triazines, Sulfonylureas	Rapeseed, Potato, Tobacco
AgraCetus, USA	Unspecified	Soybean
Allelix, Can	Atrazine, Triazines, Imidazolinone, Chlorsulfuron	Rapeseed
American Cyanamid, USA	Imidazolinone	Maize, Rapeseed
Anhauser-Bush, USA	Sulfometuron	Unspecified
ARCO, USA	Atrazine	Tomato
Bayer, FRG	Triazines	Rapeseed
Biotechnica, USA	Atrazine	Tobacco, Soybean, Rapeseed
Calgene, USA	Atrazine, Bromoxynil, Glyphosate, Phenmediphan, Phosphinotricin	Alfalfa, Tomato, Tobacco, Sunflower, Sugarbeet, Soybean, Potato, Rapeseed, Maize, Cotton, Poplar
Campbell Soup, USA	Unspecified	Tomato
Chevron, USA	Paraquat	Unspecified
Ciba-Geigy, CH	Atrazine, Metolachlor	Soybean, Sorghum, Tobacco
Diamond Shamrock, USA	2,4-D	Soybean
DNAP, USA	Sulfonylureas	Unspecified
Dow Chemicals, USA	Haloxyfop	Unspecified
Du Pont, USA	Atrazine, Picloram, Chlorsulfuron, Imidazolinone, Sulfometuron	Tobacco, Sugarcane, Soybean, Rice, Potato, Alfalfa, Oat, Maize, Carrot, Forest trees, Tomato
Eli-Lilly, USA	Trifluarin	Maize
FMC, USA	'FMC 57020'	Unspecified
Forgene, USA	Unspecified	Forest trees
Heinz, USA	Unspecified	Tomato
Hoechst, FRG	Glyphosate	Maize
ICI, UK	Glyphosate, e.o.	Maize, Sugarbeet
International Paper, USA	Unspecified	Douglas Fir

Kemira-Oy, FD	Phenmedipham	Maize, Rapeseed
Lubrizol, USA	Unspecified	Oilseed crops
Meiji Seika Kaisha Ltd., Japan	Phosphinotricin	Unspecified
Mitsui-Toatsu Chemicals, Japan	Atrazine	Rice
Mobay (Bayer) FRG	Triazines (Metribuzin)	Soybean
Molecular Genetics, USA	Chlorsulfuron, Imidazolione	Maize
Monsanto, USA	Alachlor, Glyphosate	Tomato, Tobacco, Sorghum, Rapeseed, Flax, Cotton, Maize, Soybean, Lettuce, Petunia, Sugarbeet
Nestle, CH	Unspecified	Soybean
Pfizer, USA	Unspecified	Unspecified
PhytoDynamics, USA	Glyphosate, Pendimethalin, Trifluralin	Maize, Rapeseed
Phytogen, USA	Phenmedipham	Turnip rape
Pioneer Hi-Bred, USA	Paraquat, Triazines	Maize, Alfalfa, Rapeseed
Plant Genetic Systems, B	Phosphinotricin	Sugarbeet, Tobacco, Tomato, Potato
Rhone-Poulenc, F	Bromoxinyl, Glyphosate	Soybean, Maize, Sugarbeet, Sunflower
Rohm & Haas, USA	Unspecified	Rice
Sandoz, CH	Sulfonylureas	Tobacco
Sankyo Corp., J	Atrazine	Tobacco
Schering Agrochemicals, USA	2, 4-D	Maize, Tobacco
Shell, UK/NL	Atrazine, Cinmethylin	Maize
Stauffer, USA	Thiocarbamate	Sunflower, Sorghum, Maize
Unilever (PBI, Cambridge) UK	Metolachlor, Chlortoluron	Cotton, Maize
Upjohn, USA	Unspecified	Unspecified

Part 2: Public institutions

Research by	Herbicide	Targets
Academy of Sciences, DDR	Glyphosate	Unspecified
Academy of Sciences, Hungary	Bromoxynil, Phosphino-tricin, Terbutryn, Motobromuron	Alfalfa, Tobacco
Berlin Gene-Biological Institute, FRG	2, 4-D	Unspecified
Carleton Univ., Can	Chlorsulfuron	Arabidopsis thaliana
CNRS, F	Atrazine	Unspecified
Cornell Univ., USA	Triazines, Picloram	Maize, Tobacco
Harvard Univ., USA	Atrazine	Soybean
Humbold Univ., Berlin, FRG	MCPA, Dalapon	Potato
Kebansaan Univ., Malaysia	Paraquat	Rice
Louisiana State Univ., USA	Glyphosate, Chlorsulfuron	Unspecified
MacGill Univ., Can	2, 4-D, Chlorsulfuron	Birdsfoot Trefoil
Manipur College, India	Machete, Basalin	Rice
Massachusetts Hospital, USA	Unspecified	Alfalfa
Max Planck Institute, FRG	Atrazine	Tobacco
Miami Univ., USA	Dinitroaniline	Carrot
Michigan State Univ., USA	Atrazine, Chlorsulfuron	Soybean, Aubergine, Arabidopsis thaliana
MIT, USA	Atrazine, '6 different herbicides'	Unspecified
Patricks College, Maynooth, Ireland	Chlorsulfuron, Simazine	Tobacco, Strawberry
Purdue Univ., USA	Glyphosate	Tobacco
Rothamsted Exp. Station, UK	Sulfonylureas	Unspecified
Ruhr Univ., Bochum, FRG	Glyphosate	Buckwheat
Rutgers Univ., USA	Triazines	Unspecified
Sheffield Inst. of Biotech, UK	Glyphosate	Madagascan Periwinkle
State Univ. Gent, B	Phosphinotricin	Arabidopsis thaliana

Texas Agricultural Exp. Station, USA	Atrazine	Tomato
Univ. Banaras Hindu, India	Machete, Basalin, Propanil	Microbial biofertilizers
Univ. of Alabama, USA	Atrazine	Unspecified
Univ. of Arkansas, USA	Glyphosate	Bermudagrass
Univ. of Bielefeld, FRG	Phosphinotricin	Unspecified
Univ. of Bologna, Italy	Phosphinotricin	Maize
Univ. of California (Davis) USA	Sulfometuron	Sunflower
Univ. of Chicago, USA	Atrazine	Chlamydomonas algae
Univ. of Delaware, USA	Sulfometuron	Chlamydomonas algae
Univ. of Guelph, Can	Atrazine	Rapeseed, Potato
Univ. of Hisar, India	DPX-F6025	Maize, Soybean
Univ. of Hyderabad, India	Machete, Basalin	Microbial biofertilizers
Univ. of Illinois, USA	Proline, Paraquat, Glyphosate, Atrazine	Soybean, Carrot
Univ. of Jerusalem, Israel	Sulfonylureas	Unspecified
Univ. of Kentucky, USA	Atrazine	Tobacco
Univ. of Kyoto, Japan	Atrazine	Tobacco
Univ. of Minnesota, USA	Betazone, Sethoxydim, Chlorsulfuron	Soybean, Maize, Oat, Tobacco
Univ. of Sao Paolo, Brazil	Ametryn, Dalapon	Sugarcane
Univ. of Saskatchewan, Can	Triazines, Chlorsulfuron, Glyphosate	Canola, Flax, Datura
Univ. of Tennessee, USA	Paraquat, Glyphosate	Ceratopteris ferns
Univ. of Toronto, Can	Triazines	Canola
USDA/ARS, USA	Ethofumase, Metribuzin, Atrazine	Sugarbeet, Soybean, Southernpea, Snapbean, Pepper, Tobacco, Forage and Turf Grasses
U.S. Forest Service, USA	Hexazinone, Glyphosate, Sulfometuron	Jack Pine, Poplar
Washington State Univ., USA	2, 4-D	Cowpea

Source: *Derwent Biotechnology Abstracts*, Derwent Publication Limited, London. Issues from 1986 to 1989 were scanned. Information was complemented with: Rebecca Goldburg et al., *Biotechnology's Bitter Harvest*, a report of the Biotechnology Working Group, USA, 1990; also several industrial sources were used.

by far the most researched herbicide group: 30 of the 82 groups for which herbicide tolerance is sought. Triazines have been linked to chronic health effects, such as central nervous system disorders.[20] Dangerous concentrations of atrazine were found in 29% of the samples in a US survey on surface-water quality.[21] Another six institutions are working on the old 2,4-D herbicides, suspected of causing cancer, birth defects and mutations.[22] Paraquat, probably the most toxic herbicide around for humans, is being researched for tolerance by five groups. In all, more than half of the groups listed in Table 5.1 have the old class herbicides included as targets for tolerance.

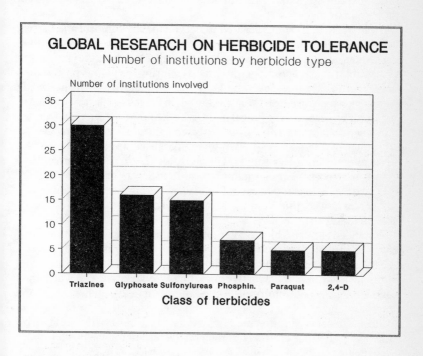

This does not mean that the newer herbicides are safe for humans and the environment. Du Pont's low-dose wheat herbicide 'Glean' is a chlorosulfuron, belonging to the group of sulfonylureas which are being researched for tolerance by at least 13 groups. Wheat is naturally immune to Glean, but other crops are not. North Dakota farmer John Leppert has experienced the consequences: 'It would be at least four years in North Dakota before a field treated with Glean could be used for some broadleaf crops.'[23] Also, American Cyanamid's new Imidazolines, used on soybean, are persistent and their residues harm other crops that follow in the cultivation cycle. Cyanamid, Du Pont and others are trying to do something about it, not by developing non-chemical weed control strategies, but by developing crops that tolerate the chemicals. Even glyphosate, which according to one Monsanto executive is so kind to the environment that it could have been 'designed by God',[24] may not be completely safe. Sold by Monsanto as 'Roundup', many of the required safety tests on this herbicide in the USA have been invalidated because of submission of misleading data on the results. Consequently, some health and safety data of this chemical are still under review. It might cause health problems due to its formulation with other ingredients, and because of possibly harmful chemical reactions in the human stomach.[25]

Apart from the obvious negative impact on the environment and the risk to human health, the increased use of herbicides can have serious indirect consequences. Research shows that some herbicides can make crops more susceptible to insect pests and diseases by altering the plant's physiology. Several crops are researched by Du Pont for tolerance to the herbicide picloram, which increases the sugar output in the roots of wheat and corn, encouraging sugar-loving fungal pathogens.[26] Another experiment showed that when maize was treated with the recommended doses of herbicide 2,4-D, for which tolerance is also being sought, it became infested with three times as many corn-leaf aphids. The maize also became more susceptible to European corn borers, corn smut disease and Southern corn leaf blight.[27] Herbicide-resistant crop lines could end up requiring more insecticides and fungicides as well, thus binding farmers even more firmly on to the pesticide treadmill.

Extended use of herbicide-tolerant crops themselves is not without risk either. Crop relatives tend to cross with each other, but also with weedy relatives that grow close by. According to crop scientist Jack Harlan, most crops have one or more sexually compatible weed relative with which they can exchange genetic information.[28] Should genetically engineered crops start handing over their herbicide-tolerant genes to weeds, the farmer is in trouble. The same gene that made it possible to use more of the same herbicide on a particular crop would then be the reason for the farmer to use even greater quantities on it, as the weeds also become tolerant.

From the TNC perspective, it is not hard to understand this heavy research emphasis on herbicide resistance. The use of herbicide-resistant crops will substantially increase the total global herbicide market, and thus the total revenues of the TNCs involved. Also an attractive prospect of herbicide-tolerance engineering is that it offers companies the possibility to bind older herbicides that go off-patent to a specific crop, thus extending the time frame of their use.[29] Another reason emerges when the costs of developing seeds and pesticides are compared. It is simply cheaper to adapt a crop to a herbicide than to develop a new herbicide. A report issued by the European Parliament puts it this way:

From the point of view of the industry, herbicide-resistant varieties are, above all, developed for economic reasons, since the development costs of a new herbicide are up to 20 times higher than those for a new variety.[30]

With both sectors often in the hands of the same TNC, the company can choose; and the choice does not seem to be difficult.

From a socio-economic and agronomic perspective, however, it is difficult to understand why scarce human resources and finance are devoted to make crops resistant to pesticides rather than to pests. With biotechnology, a further development of plant sciences could help to design herbicide-free weed control strategies. These could include better crop rotation techniques, mixed cropping systems repressing the growth of weeds, and, possibly, the use of allelopathic crops that produce natural herbicides. Biotechnology could be used together with traditional plant-breeding to help develop crop varieties that cover the soil at an early stage, thus preventing weeds from becoming a major problem. Rather than totally eliminating the weeds, which is the aim of chemical weed control, such integrated strategies focus on weed management where the farmer uses methods at his disposal to keep damage by weeds at acceptable levels.

Especially for developing countries that so desperately need low-input and locally adapted technologies for their farmers, the present priorities for biotechnology do not make much sense. As with Ciba-Geigy's 'herbishield', herbicide-resistant varieties will find their way to the Third World through the extensive distribution infrastructure of governments and TNCs. This Northern technology will, as with the Green Revolution varieties, primarily be adopted by the large farmers, resulting in a further dependence of the Third World on the North for chemical inputs. It will marginalize the rural poor who need a very different type of technology. In chapter 2, it was already explained how increased herbicide use destroys farming practices in which associated weeds are actually useful plants and form an important source of protein in the local diet and provide extra income for the village people.

Eroding the options

The focus on herbicide-tolerance does not mean that nothing is being done in other areas. Companies and public institutions are using biotechnology on different fronts in order to modify agriculture's input requirements. One of them is breeding for pest resistance. As such, this breeding objective is nothing new. Farmers have been selecting crops with resistance to insects, fungi and viruses for centuries, some of them with remarkable success. More recently, plant-breeders have been doing the same, although as noted earlier, the availability of cheap pesticides did not add to the incentives to focus on this type of research. Biotechnology now comes in as a potentially very powerful tool. Genetic engineering and tissue culture techniques allow scientists to enormously broaden the available gene pool in the search for resistance genes. No longer limited to the germplasm of sexually compatible relatives of the same species, genes can be cloned into crops from theoretically any host, be it other plants, micro-organisms or animals.

While herbicide-tolerant crops are likely to be the first genetically engineered crops available to the farmers, crops with built-in pest resistance might not take long to follow. Much of this research is being done in the public sector, but the chemical giants are also getting involved. Monsanto has already field tested a tomato incorporating genes to ward off tomato hornworms and fruit worms, as well as an engineered tomato with built-in resistance to a virus disease.[31] ICI is focusing on insect-resistant maize and virus-resistant sugar-beet,[32] and Sandoz works with PGS on virus-resistance for several crops.[33] 'Of course [the pesticides industry] is going to lose business as a result of introducing plants that are more resistant to insects or pests', says Riley from Shell Chemicals. But by investing in genetic engineering, 'we're likely to win more than we lose', he asserts.[34]

Although scientists warn that it will take several years before such new plants are available to farmers, the prospect is appealing: plants that themselves fight their enemies without need for external weapons. While the potentials are indeed enormous, the limitations are just as impressive. The resistance that biotechnology might breed into crops in the near future will be based on one or a few genes. The manipulation of entire gene complexes is still far too difficult to handle. Ed Dart, Research Director with ICI Seeds, thinks that crops with single gene traits such as insect-resistance are likely to become seed company standards during the coming decade.[35] This 'one-gene/one-pest' resistance is relatively easy to overcome by pests, which are continuously adapting themselves to new situations. Just as pests can develop resistance to pesticides, they are also able to find a way round pest-resistance in crops, especially when this resistance is provided by only one gene.

Current biotech research is heavily focused on an extremely narrow range of organisms and genes in the search for new instruments to combat pests and diseases. Graph 5.2 shows a breakdown of research reports on biological control agents as listed in *Derwent Biotechnology Abstracts* in 1989. The work on the bacteria *Bacillus thuringiensis* (Bt) is a case in point. A gene from Bt is responsible for the production of a protein that kills certain insects if they ingest it. This microbe and its 'miracle gene' is covered in over 37% of all research papers on biological control agents listed by Derwent in 1989. Another six per cent of the papers report on other *Bacillus* species, while another ten per cent focus on *Pseudomonas*, a microbe that promises to be of help in combating diseases caused by fungi. Taken together, these data suggest that over half of all listed biotech research on biological control agents focus on only two bacterial genera. And even this is probably an underestimate. As noted earlier, the *Derwent Abstracts* tend to under-represent the research in the private sector due to its secrecy. The private sector is likely to focus more strongly on those applications with clear commercial possibilities, of which Bt is the most important. Bt is, after all, responsible for 95% of all current bio-pesticide sales.[36]

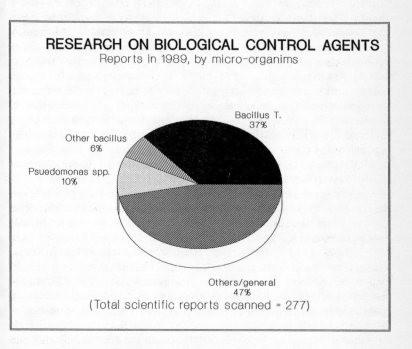

RESEARCH ON BIOLOGICAL CONTROL AGENTS
Reports in 1989, by micro-organims

Bacillus T.
37%

Other bacillus
6%

Psuedomonas spp.
10%

Others/general
47%

(Total scientific reports scanned = 277)

Engineering plants with Bt genes in them is just one of the different R&D strategies. Other strategies are the encapsulation of the toxin itself for direct use on the crop or the incorporation of the Bt gene into other microbes that naturally colonize the roots of crops or live inside the crop itself.[37] The vehicle might be different, but the 'cure' is each time the same: Bt's 'killer-gene' and the protein that it produces. Here lies exactly the danger of the cure. Researchers from the US Plant Genetic Institute have already found that several insect species can develop resistance to the Bt protein.[38] Research by Monsanto points in the same direction. With research efforts so much directed towards a single microbe, and a specific toxin of that microbe, farmers using the new crops with Bt genes in it might soon face the old problems again. Entomologist Fred Gould puts it this way:

> If pesticidal plants are developed and used in a way that leads to rapid pest adaptation, the efficacy of these plants will be lost and agriculture will be pushed back to reliance on conventional pesticides with their inherent problem.[39]

All this is not to say that the use of biotechnology to produce pest-resistant crops or 'bio-pesticides' cannot be beneficial to the farmer and to agriculture in general. We desperately need an agriculture which uses fewer harmful chemicals and other external inputs. The question is whether the current reductionist, biotech pest control approach, almost entirely focusing on single genes 'that work', is one that will help to solve the problems. The view of the biotechnologist is narrow in the sense that it focuses on solutions at the molecular level only. It is also narrow in the sense that most biotech research is dictated by commercial interests. This normally means that the solutions sought must have a global character: TNCs do not tend to work for small market niches, but aim at large market shares. The molecular mind, together with the global market share concern, leads to what is probably the most fundamental threat to sustainable low-input agriculture: uniformity.

Genetic uniformity leads to crop vulnerability. The Irish potato farmers know what that means. In the 1840s, when their staple but uniform potato crop was wiped out by blight, more than one million people died of starvation. One and a half centuries later, the US maize farmers have also learnt the hard way. In 1970, 15% of the US maize harvest was lost to the devastating effect of a little fungus-causing blight, with some states losing over half of their harvest. The cause: genetic uniformity. South-East Asian rice farmers too, using the uniform varieties from the International Rice Research Institute, can sustain their yields only with massive use of pesticides. Many ask for how long.

Whether biotechnology will help to reduce the need for chemical inputs depends, then, to a large extent on whether it will contribute to introducing more genetic diversity in the farmers' fields; in principle it can. Biotechnology opens up a tremendous pool of germplasm which earlier was not feasible for plant- and animal-breeders. Although not creating new genes as such, it provides techniques to move germplasm between organisms that do not exchange genes naturally. It also can provide for quicker germplasm identification, better storage of genetic resources and the speeding-up of plant- and animal-breeding in general.

But in the same way as biotechnology can help broaden the genetic base of our agriculture, it also has the frightening means dramatically to reduce the diversity that still remains in the farmers' fields. With the industry avid for global sales as the driving force behind the bio-revolution, increased uniformity is likely to be the dominating trend.

> Though the capacity to move genetic material between species is a means for introducing additional variation, it is also a means for engineering genetic uniformity across species

writes Jack Kloppenburg in his excellent study on the political economy of plant-breeding.[40] Another case in point is the likely widespread use of tissue culture. Through tissue culture, mass production of genetically identical plants is possible. Such cloned plants are exact copies of each other, and massive recourse to them in a certain crop would seriously increase the vulnerability of that crop. Some estimate that clonally propagated crops are six times more vulnerable to pests than their seed-bred counterparts.[41] The wide use of cloned crops will undoubtedly lead to the increased use of pesticides.

Artificial solutions?

A look beyond the horizon of the year 2000 might show an agriculture without any seed at all. 'We want something that has the ease of handling and high germination efficiency of a seed, but has the genetic uniformity of a clone', says Dennis Gray of the University of Florida.[42] Gray is working on 'artificial seeds'. Normal seed consists of an embryo (resulting from fertilization) surrounded by a reserve of the necessary starch and nutrients for germination and initial growth. Using what scientists call 'somatic embryogenesis', artificial seed technology consists of the mass multiplication of plant embryos in fermentation tanks, each of which is then encapsulated in a jelly-like coat. To some extent it is a sophisticated form of tissue culture resulting in a manageable end-product that can be stockpiled, sold and sown. The California-based biotechnology firm Plant Genetics Inc. (PGI) is generally acclaimed as the front runner in this field as it is involved both in the growing and the encapsulation of the embryos. But others are following fast (see Table 5.2). Supported with funds from the EEC Eureka project, Rhone Poulenc, Nestlé and Limagrain are involved in a joint research project on artificial tomato seed, and the Japanese giant food processor Kirin Brewery is building a special research laboratory for the purpose.

The implications are, at least in principle, enormous. The French biotechnology magazine *Biofutur* calculates that ten fermentation tanks of ten litres each can provide the whole of France with the 'seed' it needs for its entire carrot production. Some figures indicate a production of 80,000 embryos per litre per day.[43] A few tanks more, and the rest of the world is

Table 5.2
The work on artificial seeds

Research by	Crops	Comments
Agriculture Canada	Alfalfa	Also work on Brassica
Agricul. Science Inst., Korea	Celery	
Alberta Research Counc., Canada	Alfalfa	
Bhabha Atomic Centre, India	Mulberry, Sandalwood	Several research reports
Cornell Univ., USA	Soybean	
Feder. Inst. of Technol. Switzerland	Barley	Encapsulated embryos survive at least 6 months
Harima Industr. Co., Japan	Carrot	
Kemira Oy, Finland	Carrot	
Lion, Japan	Unspecified	Japan patent application for 'A new artificial seed'
Lubrizol (Sungene), USA	Barley, Rice, Sorghum, Sunflower, Wheat	Several patents for regeneration of immature embryos
Plant Genetics Inc., USA	Cauliflower, Alfalfa, Celery Brassica, Lettuce	

provided for as well. This might sound like science fiction, and to some extent it is. There are still formidable technical hurdles to be overcome. At the current state of the technology, production costs are a problem too. An average artificial seed now costs about the same as a hybrid tomato seed. Translated to major crops, however, the costs to the farmer would be exorbitant: to sow a hectare of sugar-beet, soybean or wheat with artificial seed would currently cost $4000, $13,000 and $50,000 respectively![44] This is the main reason that much of the research is currently focused on the high-value vegetable seed, such as carrot and celery. But several companies are now working on automating the methods of mass propagation, which would bring the costs down further. Encapsulated artificial seeds also provide for the opportunity further to enhance the chemical connection: Plant Genetics Inc. is working with Ciba-Geigy to encapsulate a fungicide together with the somatic embryos.

The question is not so much whether artificial seed technology will reach the farmers' fields, but when. The stakes for the industry are high. Perhaps

Purdue Research Found., USA	Carrot, Carraway	US patent application for new processes
Rhone Poulenc, France	Tomato	Eureka project, together with Nestle and Limagrain
Sinisa Stankivic Inst., Yugosl.	Horse chestnut	
Sumitomo Chemical, Japan	Rauwolfia sepentina, Chinese yam	Japan patent application for artificial seed production
Teijin, Japan	Maize, Rice, Wheat, Citrus and others	Several Japanese patent applications for methods to produce artificial seeds
Univ. of Calcutta, India	Cabbage	
Univ. of California, USA	Sugar pine, Loblolly pine, Douglas Fir	
Univ. of Florida, USA	Cantaloupe, Orchardgrass, Sweet potato	
Univ. of Guelph, Canada	Alfalfa, Brassica	Patent application for new method for artificial seeds production
Univ. of Tsukuba, Japan	Carrot	
USDA Forest Service, USA	Carrot	

Sources: *Derwent Biotechnology Abstracts*, Derwent Publication Limited, London. Issues from 1986 to 1989 were scanned; supplemented with information from: C. Fowler et al., 'The Laws of Life', in *Development Dialogue*, Dag Hammarskjold Foundation, Uppsala, No. 1–2, 1988.

the greatest danger of mass introduction of artificial seeds technology is, again, the further narrowing-down of genetic diversity, and its accompanying increase in crop vulnerability. This will undoubtedly lead to a further increase in the use of pesticides, be it of biological origin or not.

Whatever happens, use of the 'good old chemicals' in agriculture will persist for at least the foreseeable future. The chemical industries are the first to admit it. 'There certainly would not be enough food produced to feed the world without pesticides', says Reg Norman, Managing Director of Ciba-Geigy Agrochemicals. 'Without plant protection chemicals, cereal yields would drop in parts of Europe by one-quarter in the first year and by almost one half in the second', threatens the European Chemical Industry in its advertising. But the Third World needs the chemicals most, according to the industry. With stagnating sales and tighter environmental control in the North, it is the developing countries where growing markets will be found. The International Union for the Conservation of Nature (IUCN) calculates that developing countries will increase their pesticide use from some $2 billion in 1980 to over $5 billion in the year 2000.[45] It might be that resistant crops and bio-pesticides, generally designed for growing conditions in the North, manage to find their way to the farmers' plots in the foreseeable future. But the production facilities of the 'ordinary chemicals' will still be there. They might have the same fate as DDT and other chemicals: largely banned in the North but massively used in the South. An ICI spokesman puts it this way: 'Where large numbers of people are undernourished or even starving, use of plant protection chemicals can make the difference between food and starvation.'[46] It can also mean the difference between starvation and sickness, as the two million people poisoned by pesticides each year[47] might argue.

Notes and references

1. Quoted by Jack Doyle in *Altered Harvest*, Viking Press, New York, 1985, p. 90.

2. Quoted by Jack Doyle, 'Biotechnology's Harvest of Herbicides', in *Genewatch*, Vol. 2, Nos. 4–6, Boston, 1985, p. 19.

3. Schulman et al, in *Newsweek*, 18 February 1985.

4. Quoted by Jack Doyle, 1985, op. cit., pp. 109–10.

5. OTA, *Pest Management Strategies in Crop Protection*, Vol. 1, Washington, 1979.

6. OTA, quoted in Jack Doyle, 1985, op. cit., p. 190.

7. FAO, quoted in F. Wengemayer: 'Biotechnik für die Landwirtschaft aus der Sicht der Industrie', in *Entwicklung + Landlicher Raum*, Vol. 20, No. 5/85, 1985.

8. Pablo Bifani, *New Biotechnologies for Rural Development*, ILO, World Employment Programme Research, Geneva, 1989, pp. 43–4.

9. Office of Technology Assessment, *Commercial Biotechnology: an International Analysis*, OTA, Washington, 1984, p. 177.

10. Wood Mackenzie & Co., *Agrochemical Overview, 1983*.

11. *Derwent Biotechnology Abstracts*, Derwent Publications Limited, London. Issues from 1986 to 1989 were scanned.

12. Rebecca Goldburg et al, *Biotechnology's Bitter Harvest*, A Report of the Biotechnology Working Group, USA, 1990, p. 21.

13. Agricultural Genetics Report, *Du Pont and AGS Transfer Resistance to Sulfonylurea Herbicides*, Vol. 6, No. 2, April 1987, p. 1 (cited in *RAFI Backgrounder on Herbicide Tolerance*, RAFI, March 1989).

14. Personal communication to author during a biotechnology conference in Norwich, UK, December 1989.

15. Rebecca Goldburg et al, 1990, op. cit., p. 17.

16. Quoted in Jack Doyle, 1985, op. cit., p. 15.

17. Quoted in 'Agrichemical Firms Turn to Genetic Engineering', *Chemical Week*, 3 April 1985, p. 36.

18. Quoted in Jack Doyle, 1985, op. cit., p. 15.

19. M. Chiara Mantegazzini, *The Environmental Risks from Biotechnology*, Frances Pinter Publishers, London, 1986, p. 74.

20. Rebecca Goldburg et al, 1990, op. cit., p. 31.

21. Survey of US Environmental Protection Agency between 1977 and 1981, quoted in Jack Doyle, 'Herbicides of potential interest to biotechnology'. Unpublished manuscript.

22. Jack Doyle, 'Herbicides of potential interest to biotechnology', op. cit., p. 33.

23. Jack Doyle, 'Herbicides and Biotechnology: Extending the Pesticide Era.' Paper pre-

sented to a NOAH conference on biotechnology, Copenhagen, 1 November 1988, p.9.

24. 'Show Me: Monsanto's Marketing Woes', in *The Economist*, 10 March 1990.

25. Jack Doyle, 1988, op. cit., p. 18.

26. Ibid., p. 20.

27. David Pimentel, 'Down on the Farm: Genetic Engineering meets Ecology', in *Technology Review*, 24 January 1987.

28. Jack Harlan, cited in Jack Doyle, 'Biotechnology's Harvest of Herbicides', 1985, op. cit.

29. P. Niemann, 'Herbizidresistenz als Zuchtziel', in *Nachtrichenbl. Deutschen Pflanzenschutzdienst*, No. 41, Braunschweig, 1989, p. 38.

30. European Parliament, Commission on Agriculture, Fisheries and Food, 'Draft Report on the effects of the use of biotechnology', Brussels, September 1986. (Doc. PE 107.429/rev.)

31. 'Insect Resistance in Third Monsanto Field Test', in *AgBiotechnology News*, July/August 1987, p. 5.

32. 'ICI's Agbiotech Goals for the 1990s and Beyond', in *AGROW*, No. 96, 6 October 1989, pp. 5–6.

33. 'Plant Defence', Project Brief, in *The Economist Development Report*. October 1985.

34. Quoted in 'Agrochemical Firms turn to Genetic Engineering', *Chemical Week*, 3 April 1985, pp. 36–40.

35. Cited in 'ICI's Agbiotech Goals for the 1990s and Beyond', in *AGROW*, No. 96, 6 October 1989, pp. 5–6.

36. *Genetic Engineering and Biotechnology Monitor*, UNIDO, July–September 1986, p. 40.

37. 'Microbial Insecticides, Special Focus on BT', in *RAFI Communiqué*, Pittsboro, January 1989, p. 3.

38. 'Des resistance a la toxine de Bacillus', *Biofutur*, No. 89, April 1990, p. 12 (insects referred to are *Plodia interpunctella*, and *Heliothis virescens*).

39. Fred Gould, quoted in: 'Microbial Insecticides, Special Focus on BT' 1989, op. cit.

40. Jack Kloppenburg, *First the Seed*, Cambridge University Press, New York, 1988, p. 244.

41. Gordon Conway (ed.), 'Pesticide Resistance and World Food Production', cited by Pat Mooney, 'Impact on the Farm', in UNCSTD, *ATAS Bulletin*, Vol. 1, No. 1, New York, November 1984, p. 46.

42. Quoted in 'Artificial Seeds made from Clones', in *AgBiotechnology News*, 1987, p. 10.

43. C. Nouaille, V. Petiard, 'Semences Artificielles: Rêves et Réalités', in *Biofutur*, No. 67, April 1988, pp. 33–8.

44. Ibid.

45. Cited in Pablo Bifani, 1989, op. cit., p. 42. Figures refer to 90 developing countries.

46. All quotes in this paragraph are from 'Chemicals Help Feed the World'. Special advertising section of the European Chemical Industry, in *Time Magazine*, 16 October 1989.

47. Estimate for 1983 of UN Economic and Social Commission for Asia and the Pacific. Cited in Omar Sattaur, 'A New Crop of Pest Controls', in *New Scientist*, 14 July 1988, p. 49.

6. Transforming the Output

' Thanks to biotechnology it will gradually become possible to replace tropical agriculture commodities such as palm oil or manioc with products grown in the Community and other industrialized countries. This could considerably upset agricultural commodity markets and spell disaster for Third World countries dependent on them if nothing is done.'
(European Commission, 1986)[1]

'Given the technological and industrial preponderance of OECD countries (. . .) there is strong evidence that developing countries, notably those heavily engaged in agriculture, will bear the brunt of trade impacts for a long time to come.'
(OECD on impact of biotechnology, 1989)[2]

Trade has always been seen as the engine of economic growth. In early times people produced or collected food, often just the amount needed to feed themselves. As soon as people started interchanging surpluses, the very fundaments of their lives were affected. Trade introduced new commodities into their societies, changed cultural practices and power structures and created wealth and poverty depending on who was in the best position to set the conditions for the deal. In agriculture, people would produce surpluses of those crops that would grow best, and exchange them with commodities that could not so easily be produced in their region.

In later days, things started changing on a world scale, especially when the Europeans began colonizing a large part of what is now the Third World and imposing on its people the production of specific crops, the products of which were consumed back home. Today, much of the production of agricultural commodities in developing countries – especially those meant for export – is still heavily oriented towards these colonial crops. The geographical production centre of these crops often moved together with the interests of the colonial lords. Cocoa was brought into Africa from the Amazon forests, and coffee was taken from Africa to South America.

Rubber and oil-palm moved from South America to South-East Asia, and sugar-cane from Asia to the Caribbean. This reshuffling of colonial crops between Third World regions has not diminished much of their importance: today, about half of all the Third World's export income from agricultural products is derived from the mere ten crops listed in Table 6.1.

Table 6.1
Agricultural exports from the Third World
(1987, selected crops, in US$ billion)

Crop	$ billion	Share of selected countries
Coffee	9.1	Colombia and Brazil: 41%
Sugar	7.8	Cuba: 70%
Natural rubber	3.7	Malaysia and Indonesia: 70%
Cotton	3.2	Asia: 53%
Cocoa beans	2.8	Ivory Coast and Ghana: 46%
Rice	1.9	Thailand 47%
Bananas	1.8	C. America and Carib.: 56%
Tea	1.8	India, China, Sri Lanka: 70%
Oil-palm	1.8	Malaysia: 72%
Tobacco	1.7	
Top ten crops	**35.6**	
All agricultural exports	**73.6**	

Source: *FAO Trade Yearbook 1987*, FAO, Rome, 1988.

In many Third World countries these crops form the backbone of entire national economies. While an important portion of some crops, such as rice and sugar-cane, is consumed locally, the dependence on single export crops is often frightening. In 1986, three-quarters of Cuba's export income was derived from sugar, almost two-thirds of Ghana's exports from cocoa, while coffee provided Colombia with over half its income.[3]

Economists, in trying to explain production and trade patterns, have pointed to 'comparative advantage' as one of the driving forces. In agricultural production this advantage has always been predominantly formed by geographical, climatological and other agronomic factors. Coffee simply does not grow in Europe or North America, which is why coffee drinkers in the North are dependent on coffee growers in developing countries, to the value of several billion dollars a year. During the course of the 20th century, however, this comparative advantage has been progressively undermined by technology.

Agriculture has passed through its mechanical, chemical, and genetic eras, in which respectively machinery, agro-chemicals and plant breeding diminished the importance of the limitations nature puts on agricultural production. Coffee still will not grow in the North, but plant breeders managed to adapt crops to wider growing conditions. Also, the development of chemical agro-inputs reduced the importance of soil-type and of natural parasites. In developing countries, the Green Revolution is one of the prime examples of how technology has helped to diminish nature's limitations. Agricultural production has been affected by technology in other ways too: industrial production of substitutes for agricultural products, for example. Technological advances made in the chemical industry have made it possible to produce certain commodities entirely back home in the industrial countries. Synthetic rubber has displaced much of the Third World's rubber exports and chemical dyes have destroyed much of Asia's indigo production. Natural fibres have been replaced by synthetics, and pharmaceuticals are being based increasingly on industrial chemicals rather than natural resources.

Technology, then, has affected agriculture and trade in agricultural commodities for centuries. In that context, the introduction of the new biotechnologies is the continuation of an historical process. The new element is the tremendous scope of its applications and the profoundness of its implications, especially for the Third World.

Biotechnology, like many other technologies applied to agriculture, is not developed and controlled by or for the producers of agricultural commodities, but by the processors and sellers of the end product. Chemical technology made it possible to move agricultural production from its agro-ecosystems into monocultures. Biotechnology goes beyond that. It provides the tools to dissect plants into their individual genes and gene complexes, and to take production out of the arena of agriculture altogether.

Biotechnology reduces the value of plant and animal production as such and moves the dollar signs to the sub-microscopic level. Why bother with such complex structures as plants, animals and farmers, if enzymes, microorganisms and genes can do the same job? It might seem elaborate and clumsy to first extract genes from plants and animals, then incorporate them into something else, only to produce substances that have to be further modified to resemble the food that we used to eat. But the detour is logical if one takes into account by and for whom the technology is being developed. Under the control of the food processors and chemical industries, biotechnology creates a new comparative advantage, this time of industry over agriculture. In this chapter we shall look at some of the important Third World commodity crops and discuss how the new biotechnologies are affecting them.

The circle of sugar

The world's sugar comes basically from two crops: sugar-cane and sugar-beet, and one or the other of them can be grown virtually anywhere in the world. Some 60% of the world's sugar comes from cane, which is predominantly produced in the Third World. The remaining 40% is extracted from beet, grown almost exclusively in the North, especially in Europe. This makes sugar one of the agricultural commodities on which farmers in the North and South are directly competing with each other.

The history of sugar, perhaps more than any other crop, is linked to the horrors of colonialism and slavery. Originating from South-East Asia, sugar-cane found its way early – in Roman times – to the shores of the Mediterranean coast. But the real boom started only when Columbus took it to the West Indies. Later the British, Dutch and French also started planting cane in their colonies in the region, and by 1800, the Caribbean was responsible for a full 80% of the world's sugar production, a quarter of which came from the colonies of the British Empire in the region.[4] Production relied heavily on slave labour, for which more than ten million West Africans were shipped to the Caribbean. All this just to satisfy the sweet cravings of the colonizers' relatives back home, who had just learned to drink the products of some other colonial crops – tea, coffee and cocoa – to all of which sugar was added. In the 19th century sugar-cane plantations rapidly expanded into other continents and laid the basis of many developing countries' current dependence on sugar exports.

The history of sugar-beet is much shorter, but no less devastating for the cane producing countries. The beet was present in Europe from the very beginning, as it has its centre of origin in the Mediterranean region. But it was not until the beginning of the 19th century, when the Napoleonic wars kept the French blocked off from their colonies, that commercial processes were developed to refine sugar from beet. By 1880, beet had displaced cane as the principal source of sugar in Europe, and beet production spread to the USA, Canada and the USSR. By the mid-1970s, the EEC turned from sugar importer into exporter, a situation that still holds today.[5]

Only one-third of all sugar in the world enters into export statistics, the rest being consumed in the countries where it is produced. But for many developing countries sugar represents an important export. Many islands in the Caribbean, for example, export over 70% of their production and are highly dependent on this single export crop.[6] As with so many other agricultural commodities, prices of sugar on the world market fluctuate widely, making the production of sugar-cane a risky business. Since 1980, however, prices on the world market have collapsed, with little hope for recovery in the future. Production costs of sugar in, for example, the Philippines is some 12 US cents per pound, while world market prices have been below eight cents per pound since 1984.[7]

In 1985, the Prime Minister of Trinidad and Tobago summarized the predicament as follows:

If the current conditions are maintained, we shall be confronting a situation that could lead to the total destruction of the sugar industry of most developing nations, including the Caribbean basin, with all the negative consequences this will have on our economies, political stability and the security of the whole region.[8]

This statement was made at the moment when his government had to sack 8,000 sugar workers and the country's total income from trade had dropped by 60% since 1981, with sugar accounting for most of that decline. The Prime Minister's prediction was not over-dramatized: two years later the country's export income from sugar dropped an additional 38%, with many of the former sugar-workers on the verge of starvation.[9]

The picture is devastating everywhere. In the decade between 1974 and 1984, export incomes of the Group of Latin American and Caribbean Sugar Exporting Countries (GELPACEA) fell from US$6 billion to US$900 million.[10] What is bad for a country is especially bad for the poor people, in this case the sugar-cane workers. Massive unemployment, poverty and malnutrition are now hitting the workers in the cane-producing regions of the Third World.

One of the main reasons behind this disastrous situation is the EEC's sugar policy. Stimulated by the high prices the European states pay to their sugar-beet farmers – up to five times the world market price – total EEC beet production has increased substantially in the past two decades. In 1977 the European Community became a net exporter of sugar. The increasing surplus was dumped on the world market, making the EEC among the largest sugar exporters in the world. In 1986, the EEC exported more sugar than all developing countries in Africa and Asia together![11] This is probably the most important single factor in the chronically depressed world market prices for this commodity. The irony is that the European Community is constantly losing money on its dumping practices as it pays its farmers far more than what it receives on the world market.

Yet the world market is only part of the story, as some 40% of the sugar traded changes hands via special agreements. One such agreement is the Sugar Protocol of the Lomé Convention, in which the EEC agrees to buy some 1.3 million tonnes of cane each year from 17 countries in Africa, the Caribbean and the Pacific at negotiated prices which are higher than the world market. The benefits are unequally distributed, however, with only five countries (Mauritius, Fiji, Guyana, Jamaica and Swaziland) taking up over 80% of the quota.[12] But, however limited, for these countries the Lomé agreement is vital, as many of them largely depend on sugar exports. How stable this preferential treatment is, remains to be seen. Virtually all of the cane sugar sent to the EEC goes to the British sugar giant Tate and Lyle for refining. This company is the only remaining sugar-cane refiner in the UK, and finding it increasingly unprofitable to continue processing the more expensive cane sugar. If the company, which has already reduced its cane refining capacity, decides to stop refining cane altogether, the whole sugar agreement can be thrown into jeopardy and with it the livelihood of hundreds of thousands people in the Third World.

How risky such trade deals can be, is shown by the other major special agreement in sugar trade: the US quota system. To protect its domestic farmers, the United States limited cane sugar imports to specific producers, most notably the Philippines, and countries in the Caribbean and Central America. Under the quota system, these countries developed their sugar industry on the basis that their production could always be sold to the Americans. In the past decade, however, the US dramatically reduced the cane quota as domestic farmers increased production and the US food-processors increasingly switched to alternative sweeteners. While the USA imported 4.6 million tons of sugar in 1978, this figure was down to 2.5 in 1985 and to 1.6 in 1986. Some estimate that by the beginning of the 1990s, the imports will have shrunk to vanishing point.[13] The impact on those cane producers who had been made reliant on the Americans' sweet tastes, is immense. The Caribbean sugar exports to the USA fell from $686 million in 1981 to $246 million in 1984.

But perhaps no one received a harder blow than the sugar-workers in the Philippines, a country which has traditionally sent most of its sugar to the United States. Graph 6.1 shows how, within less than a decade, the country virtually lost its entire export income from this crop.[14] Two-thirds of the country's sugar comes from one island: Negros. This island soon became known as the Ethiopia of Asia. One observer reported:

> Out of a total population of two million, 250,000 are out of work. This is not just seasonal unemployment. Most of the mills have been closed down. Next year's cane has not been planted. The small planters face economic ruin, the workers starvation.[15]

Biotechnology and the new sweeteners

Sugar-cane was once known as 'The Golden Crop' due to the huge amounts of money that were made with it, although there was never much gold in sugar for the slaves of the colonial era nor for the plantation workers of today. Now, the crop is locally known as 'the hunger crop' in Brazil's cane-producing regions.[16] Not long from now the hunger crop might not exist at all, at least not as an export commodity, and only the hunger will be left.

Behind this disaster is, to a large extent, technical progress in the field of new biotechnologies, most importantly, new and improved enzyme techniques. While substitutes for sugar have been around for quite a while, only

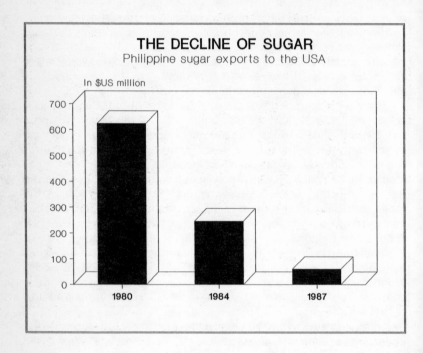

THE DECLINE OF SUGAR
Philippine sugar exports to the USA

in the last decades have scientists managed to improve production processes of the alternative sweeteners to an extent that the very existence of sugar as a commodity is at risk. By far the most important sugar substitute at the moment is High Fructose Corn Syrup (HFCS), known as isoglucose in Europe. This is developed from maize, 1.7 times sweeter than cane sugar, and currently 30% cheaper.[17] The principle of extracting sweeteners from starch has been known for quite some time, but it is the new biotechnological processes that have allowed HFCS to compete directly with sugar. The use of this sweetener increased dramatically, especially in the USA, when the soft-drink giants Coca Cola and Pepsico started shifting to HFCS in 1980. Five years later, 95% of the US non-diet, soft-drinks business used the maize-based sweeteners. In economic terms, the impact of this shift is enormous as the two soft-drink kings are together responsible for a full quarter of sugar consumption in the USA.[18] Combined with similar shifts by the food processing industries, this has been the most important single factor behind the drastic US sugar import quota cuts from the Caribbean and the Philippines described above. After having switched to HFCS, Coca Cola now markets its products in the Third World with the slogan 'Hope for the future'. Hope for whom?

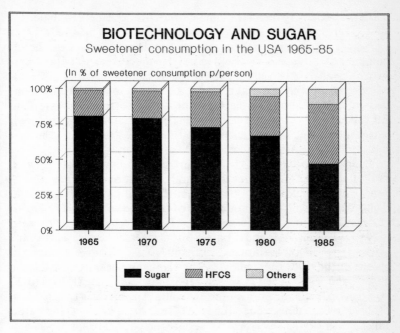

BIOTECHNOLOGY AND SUGAR
Sweetener consumption in the USA 1965-85

(In % of sweetener consumption p/person)

Legend: Sugar, HFCS, Others

Japan's food-processors are also working on HFCS technology and already producing 11 per cent of the world market, but massive use of the sweetener has been limited, as Japan imports virtually all its maize. For the moment, the expansion of the corn sweeteners in the EEC has been restricted due to the strong lobby of the sugar-beet producers and industry.

While some estimate that the current six million tonnes of HFCS produced worldwide (of which the USA uses three quarters)[19] is the maximum the market can take, food-processors are using biotechnology to further expand and speed up the substitution process. Until recently, CS was only available in liquid form, thus limiting its use to processed food and soft drinks. This was until the US company Staly Continental announced that it had developed a technique to crystallize HFCS, and started marketing its new sweetener 'Crystar' in 1987.[20] It is estimated that the crystallized fructose will capture a further half a million tonnes of the market away from sugar by 1990.[21] The OECD already talks of 'further waves of substitution . . . with inroads being made into domestic sugar consumption.'[22] As the OECD further points out, the maize-based sweetener is just one example of the substitution, as similar technologies are being developed to derive sweeteners from a whole range of crops. In that context, it might be better to talk about 'starch derived sweeteners',[23] as starch from potatoes and other crops is also being converted in the same way as starch from corn.

Dramatic enough in their implications, the starch sweeteners are just the tip of the iceberg. In their interminable search for cheaper raw materials, the food-processors are hunting for sweeteners which are hundreds or even thousands of times sweeter than sugar while containing no calories. The first commercial successes in this field came from the chemical laboratories in which scientists constructed, combined and recombined molecules that could compete with sugar. Aspartame, a non-caloric chemical sweetener, was one of the first commercial breakthroughs. In search of a share of the cake, several companies are now wielding biotechnology tools to improve aspartame production with enzymes and microbes. Table 6.2 lists the main industrial actors in the hunt for alternatives to sugar.

But people no longer like chemicals in their food, and the real challenges of the future lie in the hunt for the natural non-calorie sweeteners and the genes which produce them. This hunt leads the food-processors back to the Third World where plants produce incredibly sweet compounds. The case of thaumatin has been well documented.[24] *Thaumatococcus danielli*, locally known as katemfe, is found in humid forest zones in Western and Central Africa and produces the protein thaumatin, some 2,500 times sweeter than sugar.[25] In the 1970s Tate and Lyle set up plantations of katemfe in Ghana, Liberia and Malaysia.[26] The frozen berries are sent to the UK where the company extracts and purifies the thaumatin protein which is then sold as 'Talin' for, according to one estimate, $US16,500 per kilo.[27] As the extraction process is extremely expensive, several companies are now working to produce the sweetener in the laboratory, using genetic engineering and enzyme technology. Unilever was the first company that managed to isolate the gene coding for thaumatin and to insert it into the bacteria *E. coli*. Later, researchers at the University of Kent (UK) extracted it and inserted it into tobacco.[28] Tobacco might not seem an obvious choice, but this opens the way to inserting the sweet gene into a whole range of edible crops. These crops might be used as biological 'factories' to produce larger quantities of the desired product in a more convenient crop. They might also be used to produce naturally sweet food crops – avoiding the need to add sugar to the end product.

Since 1982, Beatrice Food (USA) has been funding research at Ingene Inc. (a US biotechnology company), which resulted in the cloning of the gene out of katemfe and into yeast strains. Beatrice holds the patents on the process and it is estimated that the company will earn up to US$25 million in royalties.[29] One drawback of thaumatin is that it has a lingering aftertaste, which limits its use to specific products, but officials from Tate and Lyle claim that protein engineering can change this and widen the possible applications of this sweetener.[30] It appears that it is just a question of time for the food-processors to commercially produce thaumatin from microbes in fermentation tanks, or directly in the edible plants themselves, which would eliminate the need for the current Tate and Lyle plantations in the Third World. The resulting decrease of production costs would put this new

Table 6.2
The attack on sugar: biotechnology research on the new sweeteners

Research by	Research on
Ajinomoto, Japan	New enzyme technology for aspartame production, also work on Lippia sweeteners
Asahi Chemicals, Japan	New enzyme technology for aspartame production
Beatrice Foods, USA	Monoclonal antibodies to bind thaumatin, also enzymatic work on thaumatin. Several patents
Bioeurope, France	Aspartame production with new enzymes, several patents. Research for Hoechst, FRG
Blaise Pascal University, France	Aspartame production with enzyme technology
Centro del CNR, Milano, Italy	Aspartame production using penicillin enzymes
CSIRO, Australia	Enzyme technology for aspartame production
Dainippon, Japan	Stevioside sweetener production and modification with microbes
Daiwa Chemicals, Japan	Sweetener production from starch with microbes
Delft University, Netherlands	Sweetener production using modified yeasts
Enzyme Bio Systems, USA	Sweeteners with new enzyme technology, EPO patent application
Genencor, USA	Aspartame production with new enzyme technology
Hiroshima University of Medicine, Japan	Tissue culture for sweeteners from Stevia sp.
Ingene, USA	rDNA thaumatin genes expressed in yeasts, contract research for Beatrice Foods
Kyoto University, Japan	Sweetener production with yeasts
Lotte Inc.	Fructose production using microbes, patent applications in Japan
Lucky-Biotech, USA	Monellin substitutes from rDNA cell cultures
Meiji-Sheika, Japan	Sweetener production using microbes and plants
Michigan Biotech. Institute, USA	Improvement HFCS production with enzymes
Mitsubishi Chemicals, Japan	New sweeteners from starch
Mitsui Sugar, Japan	New sweeteners from microbes and enzymes
Morita Chemical Co., Japan	Stevia tissue culture for better sweeteners. Patent applications in Japan
Nabisco, USA	Enzyme technology for fructose sweetener production

Nippon Food, Japan	New enzyme technology for sweetener from starch
Nippon Tobacco, Japan	Stevioside modification with microbes
NOVO Industries, Denmark	Sweeteners from maize with enzymes
Queens University Ontario, Canada	New sweeteners with enzyme technology
Science University of Tokyo, Japan	New sweeteners with enzyme technology
Shakai Chemical Industries, Japan	Sweetener extraction from mulberry tree
Showa, Japan	Aspartame production with different microbes. Also sweeteners from starch with yeasts and enzymes
Tate & Lyle, UK	New enzyme technology for new sweeteners. Also work on thaumatin and aspartame
Toyo-Soda, Japan	Aspartame production using microbes (Pseudomonas sp.) and enzymes
Unilever, UK	Thaumatin genes expressed in microbe (E. coli)
University of California, USA	Monellin substitutes from rDNA cell cultures
University of Kent, UK	Thaumatin genes expressed in tobacco
University of London, UK	Analysis of sweet proteins in Thaumatin sp.
USDA, USA	New sweeteners from microbes
WR Grace, USA	New sweeteners with enzyme technology, including aspartame. Several patent applications

Sources: *Derwent Biotechnology Abstracts*, Derwent Publication Limited, London. Issues from 1986 to 1989 were scanned. Also numerous industry publications were scanned for this table.

sweetener in more direct competition with sugar, thus further aggravating the sugar crisis.

Thaumatin is just one of the new plant sweeteners that threaten the future of sugar; Table 6.3 lists some others. The sweetener hunters ransack savannas, tropical forests and deserts in search of plants and genes that produce even sweeter proteins. The Japanese found an excellent candidate in *Stevia rebaudiana*, which grows in Paraguay and several countries in South-East Asia. The *Stevia* proteins are several hundred times sweeter than sugar and are already being marketed in Japan by a subsidiary of Suzuki Int'l (called Stevia Company), together with Morita Chemical Company. Again, a problem that limits its market is that some of the *Stevia* sweeteners

Table 6.3
The natural super sweets

Sweetener	Plant	From	Sweetness
Thaumatin	Katemfe (T. danielli)	W. Africa	2500 times sugar
Monellin	Serendipity berry	W. Africa	3000 times sugar
Miraculin	Miraculous berry	W. Africa	
Steviocides	Bertoni (Stevia rebaudiana)	Paraguay	300 times sugar
Hernandulcin	Lippia dulcis	Mexico	1000 times sugar
Peviandrin	Brazilian licorice	Brazil	
Glucosides	Several medicinal plants	China	
Mogroside	'Lo han kuo'	China	
	Momordica grosvenori	China	
Glycyrrhizin	Licorice		
Phyllodulcin	Hydrange		

Sources: *Derwent Biotechnology Abstracts*, Derwent Publication Limited, London, issues from 1986 to 1989 were scanned; A. Sasson, *Biotechnology and Development*, UNESCO, Paris, 1988; C. Juma, *The Gene Hunters*, Zed Books, London, 1989.

has a bitter after-taste. Companies are using microbes and enzyme technology to change this. Another parallel approach is to select *Stevia* plants with a higher content of the non-bitter proteins. The Hiroshima Medical School pioneered the tissue-culture work, after which the Suzuki subsidiary man aged to produce tissue-cultured *Stevia* varieties which can grow in the USA, and produce less of the bitter proteins. Again, it seems a question of time until the companies disregard the plant and manage to produce *Stevia* proteins commercially with microbes and enzymes.

In roughly the same African regions where the thaumatin producing katemfe grows, you can find the 'Miraculous Berry', which produces a sweet protein called Monellin. The protein is 3,000 times sweeter than sugar, and North American scientists from the University of California are already trying to produce this extremely sweet substance via genetically-engineered cell cultures. The list seems endless. Scientists from Illinois University in Chicago plunged into old Mexican botanical literature and found a plant one thousand time sweeter than sugar (*Lippia dulcis*). The Mexican Indians enjoyed chewing it even before the Aztecs arrived. Some Chinese medicinal plants were scanned and found to be extremely sweet, as was also the case with Brazilian liquorice.

The search for the sweet genes from the South might bring us back to the beginning of the sugar-circle, which started at the end of the 15th century when Columbus introduced sugar-cane into the Caribbean. The history of sugar, from a curious sweet crop in Polynesia, via the plantation horrors of the high tide of slavery, into the current sugar crisis, might end with a few sweet genes, also from the Third World, which finally make it possible to reduce Northern dependence on yet another crop from the South.

The chocolate crop

The history of cocoa is fascinating. Perhaps no other agricultural commodity has travelled so much around the globe. In international trade, cocoa was a late starter, but now it is one of the most important agricultural commodities that the South trades with the North. Cacao is indigenous to the Amazon basin of South America, but the Spaniards also found it in Central America, where the Aztecs were using the bean in religious ceremonies. Until the early 19th century cacao consumption remained largely confined to Spaniards who at that time ate and drank a full one-third of the global production. Production was logically confined to the Spanish colonies in Latin America, notably Venezuela, which at the beginning of the 19th century accounted for half of global production. Somewhat later, the Portuguese started to plant cacao in Brazil, and only by the end of the 19th century did the French, Germans and British start planting it in their African colonies. This marked the beginning of a shift in production from Latin America to Africa. While in 1900 some 85% of world production came from Latin America, it was Africa which, by the 1960s, provided some 75% of the world's cocoa.[31]

The future looked bright for the African cocoa producers, as cocoa prices rose considerably from some $0.30 per pound in the 1960s[32] to the historic $1.72 in 1977.[33] A few African countries, notably Ivory Coast, Ghana, Cameroon and Nigeria, became heavily dependent on this single crop, and together these four countries provided 65% of global cocoa production. But golden years never last long. Encouraged by the high prices, countries in Latin America, especially Brazil, started planting massively and so did Malaysia on the other side of the globe. Between 1980 and 1987, Brazil increased its area planted with cocoa by over one-third, while Malaysia almost quadrupled its cocoa plantations in the same period. Of the African countries, only Ivory Coast managed to increase its acreage under cocoa.[34] Global production jumped from 1.4 billion tonnes in 1970 to some two billion in 1988, while consumption increased only marginally.[35] The chronic over-production resulted in steadily falling prices – often below the costs of production – and declining export incomes. Some important figures on world cocoa production and trade are given in Table 6.4. Graphs 6.3 and 6.4 show how world production of this crop has shifted during the 1970s and 1980s.

The figures indicate a tremendous shift of cocoa production away from Africa within the past two decades. Despite expansion of production in the Ivory Coast, Africa's share of global cocoa production dropped from 71% in 1970 to a projected 54% in 1990. Production is moving back to Latin America (Brazil), from where it came a century ago, but also into Asia (Malaysia) which increased its market share from virtually nothing in 1970 to some 12% by 1990.

This time, however, it is not the colonial landlords who decide from

Table 6.4
Cocoa production, yield, exports and dependency

	Production 1987 (1000 MT)	% Change[1] 1980/1987	Yield 1987 (KG/HA)	Exports 1987[2] (MIL. $)	Dependency on cocoa exports[3]
Cameroon	120	0%	267	237	52%
Ghana	210	–22%	175	489	99%
Ivory C.	570	21%	543	1084	57%
Nigeria	130	–23%	186	168	73%
Brazil	405	23%	622	606	7%
Malaysia	175	361%	1072	344	9%
Other Third W.	392	32%	308	867	1%
Third W. total	**2002**	**18%**	**369**	**3795**	**5%**

Notes:
1 Refers to change in total cocoa production since 1980
2 Export income includes (semi)processed cocoa products
3 Dependency is measured export income from cocoa per income from export of all agricultural products

Source: FAO, *1987 Production and Trade Yearbooks*, FAO, Rome, 1988.

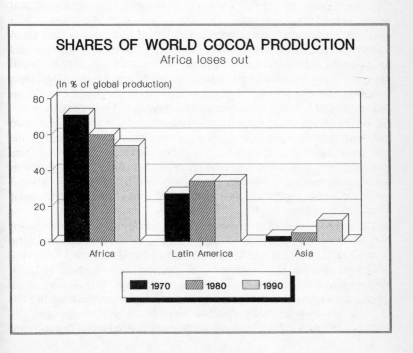

SHARES OF WORLD COCOA PRODUCTION
Africa loses out
(In % of global production)
Africa   Latin America   Asia
1970   1980   1990

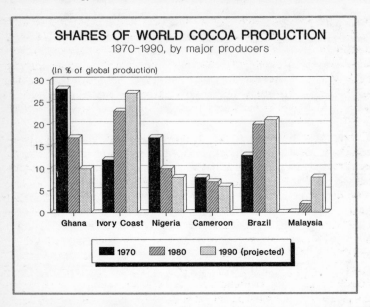

where the bulk of the production comes; at least, not in the straightforward way this happened in the 19th century. An increasingly important factor in who is able to reap the benefit this time is technology. While in the 1970s production increases were largely the result of area expansion, an increasingly important factor now is yield. Malaysia, for example, harvests almost twice as much cocoa from a hectare as does Brazil, and up to six time more than Ghana or Nigeria. One key to these differences is technology, especially the use of new hybrid varieties, fertilizer, pesticides and irrigation. The other key is scale: Malaysia, and to a somewhat lesser extent Brazil, produce much of their cocoa output on large plantations, while the African counterparts rely more on small, farmer-based production.[36] Much of the spectacular decline of Ghana's and Nigeria's share in the world's cocoa production is due to the fact that small farmers have not been able to incorporate new hybrids and other inputs into their production systems.

In Brazil, the gap between modernized plantations and the position of small farmers is especially apparent. Ninety per cent of Brazil's cocoa production comes from the Bahia province in the north-east,[37] where some 20,000 small farmers, using traditional trees, produce alongside modernized plantations which provide jobs for over 100,000 workers.[38] To expand cocoa production, Brazil started to set up new plantations in the 1970s. While the plantations boosted Brazil's total cocoa output, a decline in total production in the Bahia region is foreseen.[39] The modernization process brought about a tremendous concentration of land ownership and income, which led to many small cocoa farmers being pushed out of business and forced to work on the plantations. Between 1970 and 1980, the proportion of waged labourers versus small independent farmers in the region had doubled.[40] The collapse of cocoa prices in 1988 – the lowest for 14 years, with no signs of recovery [41] – will cost Brazil an expected $170 million in export earnings, but might also cost the livelihood of thousands of small, cocoa growers and farm workers in the Bahia region.[42]

On 30 March 1988, Bra Kanon, the Ivory Coast's Minister of Agriculture, responded to the cocoa crisis by announcing that his country would no longer develop new land for cocoa production but instead turn to extending coffee, palm-oil and rubber acreages. The largest cocoa producer in the world was losing one dollar on each kilogram of cocoa sold.[43] Kanon denounced industrialized countries for keeping cocoa prices down in search of 'exploitation, superexploitation, profit, superprofit'.[44] At about the same time, on the other side of the globe, however, an official from Kumpulan Guthrie announced it was substantially expanding its cocoa plantations. Kumpulan Guthrie is one of the Malaysia's largest plantation companies, controlling over 100,000 plantation hectares. The reason, according to a company official: 'our ability to compete from a position of strength in biotechnology'.[45]

Current biotechnology research relevant for cocoa can roughly be divided into two types. On the one hand, biotechnology is used to create higher yielding cocoa hybrids allowing developing countries to produce more of this precious commodity and the TNCs to get their raw material cheaper. On the other, dollars are poured into research to create high quality substitutes for cocoa-butter from other sources, resulting in a gradual elimination of the need to use cocoa beans for the production of chocolate.

Increasing the yield

Genetic research on cocoa has already resulted in the production of new hybrids which produce considerably more than the traditional trees. The enormous yield differences between Malaysian and Ghanaian cocoa trees are an indication of this. Traditional plant-breeding in cocoa is, however, extremely painstaking as it takes several years before the trees mature and are ready for crossing and back-crossing. Tissue culture could speed up this process enormously and, additionally, provide the basis for introducing genetic changes at the cellular level. Tissue culture would also hasten the dissemination of already existing superior cocoa varieties. Up to now scientists have not succeeded in developing tissue-culture techniques that can be used commercially, but those working on it are confident that this will be possible in the near future.[46] Hershey Foods has already filed a patent application at the European Patent Office in which it claims a method for the production of 'genetic carbon copies' of cocoa plants, using culture.[47]

Many of the most important TNCs processing cocoa are either conducting or funding biotechnology research in this area, including Hershey Foods

(USA), Cadbury-Schweppes (UK), Nestlé (Switzerland) and Mars Inc. (USA). These four companies are among the nine TNCs that control 80% of world production of chocolate and other cocoa products.[48] The interest of the cocoa processing TNCs is obvious. Now depending on a narrow range of cocoa-producing countries, and highly susceptible to weather conditions, diseases and political circumstances, TNCs are eager to find a stable supply of cocoa beans from well-run plantations. When commercially available, the result of tissue-culture techniques will undoubtedly be a further shift of cocoa production to large plantations, a process that has been taking place during the 1970s and 1980s, but which will be further intensified. Small farmers in Africa and Brazil's north-east will simply not have the means and inputs necessary for the new hybrids, as is already the case. Consequently, it will also enhance the current trend of a further decline in Africa's share of world cocoa production, as these countries do not have the infrastructure in place to cope with the new technology.

The hunt for substitutes

> *'There are many different kinds of chocolate but no matter how sweet or bitter it is all chocolate starts with cocoa beans.'* (in an educational book for children)[49]

Biotechnology may mean that we have to change the stories we tell to our children. One angle from which cocoa is being attacked by biotechnology is in the production of cocoa-butter substitutes (CBS). The use of cocoa substitutes in chocolate and related products is not new, and certainly not limited to developments in biotechnology; but biotechnology promises to make a major contribution to the production of higher quality substitutes.

Today, global production of CBS is some 200,000 tonnes, of which only 50,000 are of high quality. This roughly corresponds to half a million tonnes of cocoa beans, which is a quarter of world cocoa bean production. Interestingly, the main drive for cocoa substitutes comes not from the chocolate manufacturers, but rather from the edible oils industry; Unilever and Fuji Corp. are the world's largest CBS producers.[50] Both are using biotechnology to produce cocoa butter from cheaper oils, as do other food-processors. Table 6.5 lists the major actors in the hunt for substitutes. Depending on quality, CBS can come from the whole range of crops that produce oil-seeds, and even fish and whale oil are being used. The main bottleneck to further progress is the limitation of the currently used methods to isolate specific fractions from different oils for the CBS production. Improved enzyme techniques and genetic engineering of the fermentation microbes are, however, already resulting in giant leaps forward towards the successful imitation of cocoa.

Again, the main interest of the industry in conducting this type of

Table 6.5
Biotechnology research on cocoa

Research by	Type of research	Comments
Penn State Univ. (USA)	Tissue culture for HYVs, increasing fat content, incorporating 'sweetness genes'. Also rDNA work on cocoa tree	$1.5 million budget, co-funded by industry (ACRI and US Chocolate Manufacturers Association)
DNAP (USA)	Tissue culture for new varieties	Joint venture research with Hershey Foods. EPO patent application filed for cocoa TC technique
Cadbury-Schweppes (UK/USA)	Tissue culture and rDNA. Also work on improving fermentation of cheap cocoa	With University of Reading (UK). Tissue culture research has reportedly stopped recently
Ajinomoto (Japan)	CBS from cheap oils	Licensed patent from Tokyo University
Fuji Oil (Japan)	CBS from olive, safflower or palm-oil	Processes patented. Company claims the CBS has good properties for chocolate
CPC Int'l (USA)	CBS from yeasts	Process patented
Genencor (USA)	Enzyme techniques to convert palm-oil in cocoa butter	Patent application for process filed
Cornell Univ. (USA)	Cell culture to produce CBS	Research started in 1987
Nestlé (CH)	Enzyme techniques to improve fermentation of cheap cocoa	Focus on cheap cocoa from Malaysia
Mars (UK/USA)	Enzyme techniques to improve taste of Malay cocoa, including fermentation techniques	Joint research with Malaysian government
KAO Corp. (Japan)	rDNA enzymes to produce CBS	Two patent applications at EPO
Unilever (UK)	Enzyme technology to convert several oils and fats into CBSs	Unilever currently controls 50% of global CBS market

Wessanen (Netherl.)	CBS from mutant yeasts	Dutch patent application for new techniques. Company claims that new method is fast and economical
Station des Cultures Fruitières (Belgium)	Tissue culture of cocoa	100% of regeneration rate is claimed
USDA/ARS (USA)	CBS from cottonseed and olive oil	
IAEA/FAO (Austria)	Tissue culture of cocoa	
University of Lille (France)	Growth regulators and tissue culture on cocoa tree	
Univ. of Manchester (UK)	Protoplast isolation and fusion	
Univ. of Liverpool (UK)	Protoplast isolation	

Sources: H. Svarstad, *Biotechnology and the International Division of Labour*, Oslo University, December 1988; *Derwent Biotechnology Abstracts*, Derwent Publication Limited, London. Issues from 1986 to 1989 were scanned.

research is obvious. The substitutes come from cheaper and more reliable sources. Oil-palm, producing the cheapest vegetable oil around, is a main candidate. But also the oils and fats of crowps that grow well in the North are being converted. Chang, working for USDA/ARS, reports work on cotton-seed and olive oil,[51] and in European patent applications safflower, sunflower, soybean and rape-seed are mentioned as possible competitors with cocoa.[52] But the research does not stop there. Apart from converting plant-produced vegetable oils, biotechnology also opens up ways for cocoa to be produced by micro-organisms – doing without plants altogether. Wessanen, a Dutch subsidiary company of the UK-based Berisford, has filed several patent applications in the Netherlands for a technique to produce cocoa-butter substitutes using different yeast strains.[53] CPC International, in the USA, holds a patent on a process to produce cocoa-butter substitutes with yeast.[54] Fuji Oil, in Japan, is developing techniques to do the same with other microbes.[55]

It will take some time, but slowly and quietly the world's main food-processors are making it possible to decrease the need for real cocoa beans for the production of chocolate and related products. Biotechnology is the key factor to this. Current legislation in different countries, specifying how much 'natural cocoa' should be in products called chocolate, is hardly seen as an impediment. Within the EEC, for example, these requirements are continually debated under strong lobby pressure from the chocolate and edible oils industries to liberalize them.[56] Whether the cheapest technique will finally be to obtain substitutes from yeasts, from bacteria, from cultured cells or from oil-seeds makes hardly any difference to the small cocoa farmers of Africa, Brazil, or anywhere in the developing world. With the large plantations stepping-up their production and the giant food companies looking for other raw materials, the current cocoa crisis seems far from over. In the past two decades, policy makers at the international level have tried four times to guarantee stable and reasonable prices in the context of the International Cocoa Agreement. None of the attempts really worked. Diverging interests of producer and consumer countries rendered most of the attempts useless even before the negotiations had started. Biotechnology is bound to complicate matters even more. Differentiated access to the technology within the producers' block is already resulting in different interests as well.

The battle for vegetable oils

The international situation with respect to vegetable oils is highly complex and its future hard to predict. According to FAO, total production of vegetable oils virtually doubled between 1972 and 1990,[57] with 95% coming

Table 6.6
Global vegetable oil production and exports

	Global Production		Global exports	Third World exports	
	Mill mt.	Share	Mill. mt.	$ million	Share
Soybean oil	15.0	30%	6.1	574	15%
Palm-oil	8.5	17%	5.2	1789	48%
Rapeseed oil	6.5	13%	1.7	39	1%
Sunflower oil	6.7	13%	2.1	226	6%
Coconut oil	3.1	6%	1.7	534	14%
Cottonseed oil	3.1	6%	0.3	37	1%
Groundnut oil	3.7	7%	0.6	153	4%
Olive oil	1.8	4%	0.3	149	4%
Palm kernel oil	1.3	3%	0.7	232	6%
Total 9 crops	**49.7**	**100%**	**18.7**	**3733**	**100%**

Note: Figures are for 1987, except 'Global Exports' for 1986.

Sources: *FAO Commodity Review and Outlook 1987–88*, Rome, 1988; *FAO Trade Yearbook 1987*, Rome, 1988.

from just nine crops, with soybean, palm, sun-flower and rape-seed accounting for slightly less than three-quarters of the total. With oil-palm being cultivated exclusively in the South, and soybean, rape-seed and sun-flower in both industrialized and developing countries, vegetable oil is a truly global commodity with both the North and the South competing for the same market. Although only one-third of the total production is exported (the rest consumed domestically), vegetable oils form an important source of income for developing countries, totalling some $3.7 billion in 1986.

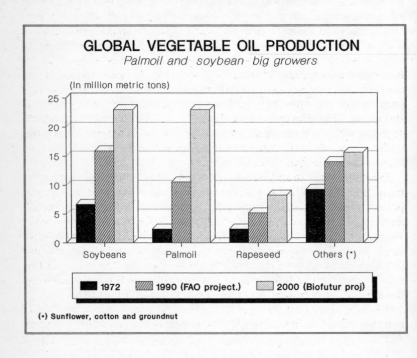

GLOBAL VEGETABLE OIL PRODUCTION
Palmoil and soybean big growers

(In million metric tons)

1972 · 1990 (FAO project.) · 2000 (Biofutur proj)

(•) Sunflower, cotton and groundnut

As with most other agricultural commodities, the export incomes are highly concentrated within specific countries. Most of the money made on exporting palm-oil goes to Malaysia, while virtually all the soybean oil income of the Third World goes to Brazil and Argentina. Three-quarters of the world coconut oil exports are from the Philippines.[58] Oil from these three crops provides a full three-quarters of all Third World export revenues from vegetable oils, with the unquestionable trade champion being the oil-palm. This is not to say that exports of vegetable oil are irrelevant for other developing countries, or that other vegetable oil crops are not important. In several cases they form a very important source of income, especially for African countries.

The share of different oil crops in world production changed dramatically during the 1970s and 1980s. The big growers were oil-palm and soybean with rape-seed as a good third. Together they moved from 39% to 55% of the global market share between 1972 and 1990.[59] A look into the future confirms this tendency to concentration in the vegetable-oil race. *Biofutur* projects that just after 2000, palm-oil production will have jumped to a staggering 23 million tons a year, almost three times its 1987 output, and soybean will reach the same level. Rape-seed will jump to some eight million tons, while the output of the other oil crops will increase only slightly or remain static[60] (see Graph 6.5).

Oil-palm, soybean and rape-seed also happen to be the major targets for biotech research. What the three crops have in common is that they fit perfectly into large-scale, high-tech agriculture. Palm-oil comes mainly from large plantations in South-East Asia. More than half the world's soybean production comes from farmers in the United States, and the same share of global rape-seed production comes from European and Canadian fields. Biotechnology will help modify these crops and their oils to further enhance their productivity in large-scale production. It will also allow for the substitution of tropical oils by their Northern counterparts.

Biotechnology work on oil-palm has been described in depth by RAFI[61] and Sasson.[62] Most of the research focuses on commercial tissue culture. According to Unilever, the main actor in this field, this could result in yield increases of 30% and more. Since 1970, the French Institute for Oils and Fats (IRHO) together with their colleagues from the Institute of Scientific Research for Development Co-operation (ORSTOM), have been developing techniques for cloning oil-palm. By 1984, the two research organizations had planted 50,000 oil-palm clones in the Ivory Coast. Contracts were also signed with plantation companies in Malaysia and Indonesia to provide respectively 3.5 million and 2.6 million cloned plantlets annually.[63] Separately, Unilever has developed techniques to clone oil-palms and created a production capacity of over half a million clones annually in its laboratories in the UK and Malaysia. The company has also started planting in Colombia and Brazil, and predicts that by 1995 it will earn about $25 million from selling oil-palm clones.[64] But technical problems occurred. The Unilever clones planted in Malaysia in 1983, produced flowers that functionally were neither male nor female, and the fruits were aborted.[65]

Despite Unilever's initial problems, efforts to clone oil-palm continue and are expected dramatically to influence world vegetable-oil production. Different trees on the same plantations can have substantial yield variations. With cloning, the highest yielding trees can be selected from an otherwise heterogeneous population and copied: the outstanding becomes the norm. Should scientists manage to perfect the technique, the current yield of two to five tonnes per hectare could more than double to 10 to 12, according to some estimates.[66] Enthusiastic about the bright future of this crop, planters in Malaysia are now switching from rubber to oil-palm. In a spectacular bid to grab an increasing share of the world market, neighbouring Indonesia is embarking on a massive planting programme and projects to increase its acreage under palm-oil to two million hectares in 1995.[67] Countries in Latin America have increased their production by 150% since 1980[68] and plan to go further still.

With all this expanded production, a collapse in prices was inevitable. When it came, in the second quarter of 1986, it was spectacular – prices crashed to less than a third of the previous year. Prices recovered somewhat in 1987, but have remained extremely poor by historical standards. The promise of future yield increases from biotechnology might turn into a disaster, especially for the small farmers in the business. Only the large plantations will be able to bear the additional costs of the cloned palms which require considerably greater management and up to six times more pesticides.[69] But the biotechnological aided oil-palm boom will also have a profound impact on producers of other vegetable oils, such as coconut and ground-nut.

For illustration, let us examine a country such as the Philippines. It is estimated that about 25% of the total population of this country is wholly or mainly dependent on the coconut palm (cultivation, processing industry, transport, marketing). While oil-palm is a typical large estate crop, coconut is grown mainly by the 700,000 small Filipino coconut farmers. They are not able to replant more productive varieties when prices are low. In the past, the exports of coconut products brought in between 15% and 20% of the country's total export earnings. Because of declining productivity and decreasing prices, the export earnings dropped from $1 billion in 1979 to $555 million in 1984, and in 1985 this figure had dropped further to $353 million. The position of the millions of Filipinos depending on this sector is in danger and the lack of alternative employment is leading to enormous increases in poverty.[70] Yet the real 'palm-oil boom', resulting in ever-sinking prices and an increasing market share for palm-oil, has still to come.

Even for a major palm-oil producing country like Malaysia the impact has negative aspects. Malaysia depends to a large extent on two agricultural commodities: oil-palm and rubber. Growing oil-palm has become more attractive than growing rubber because of the increased yields, resulting in a massive switch from rubber to oil-palm. Rubber plantations, however, are more labour intensive than oil-palm. Accordingly, the switch will reduce the demand for labour, threatening the employment of hundreds of thousands of plantation workers on the rubber estates. At the moment this loss seems to be compensated by a spectacular expansion of cocoa plantations.[71] But cocoa, as explained earlier in this chapter, is also threatened by substitution.

While it is true that unrefined palm-oil is often an important source of food in areas where the tree is cultivated, it remains to be seen whether biotechnology will help to improve the nutritional value of this traditional food source. The potential is there, but Unilever's efforts seem to point to another more lucrative direction: 'An important long-term goal is to modify the fatty acid composition of oil-bearing seeds to make them ideally suited to manufacturing purposes.' Not nutritional value but 'obviating the need for costly chemical or enzyme processing' is Unilever's main in using biotechnology to change the components in oil-palm seeds.[72]

But then, biotechnology is not only swinging the vegetable oil balance from Third World small-scale producers to plantation companies in the South, it also will help the North to become self-sufficient in its vegetable oil requirements. A case in point is current biotechnology research on rape-seed. Although China and India are major cultivators of this crop, most of the world's rape-seed is produced in the North, especially Western Europe and Canada. The EEC, highly dependent on vegetable oil imports, heavily subsidizes domestic cultivation of rape-seed. The problem with this crop is the composition of its oil, a factor which many companies and institutions are now working on. The biotechnology company Calgene intends to get rape-seed to yield 'high-priced specialty oils that are currently derived principally from coconut and palm kernel.'[73] Unilever is also using biotechnology to modify the oil content of rape-seed,[74] as are several other food-processors. Research in Canada points in the same direction. Traditional plant breeding has already helped to improve the position of rape-seed as an edible oil producer by reducing toxic oil components of the crop. Biotechnology will further improve the process and put the crop in a better position *vis-à-vis* competing ones from the South.

Scientists are already working towards producing edible oil by way of microbes, on a commercial scale: the so-called Single Cell Oils (SCO). Based on the genetic modification of yeasts, bacteria, fungi or algae, which feed on a whole range of different substrates, the SCO technology is currently still too expensive to compete with vegetable oils such as oil-palm and soybean. But this might change in the future. Scientists from Henkel Company propose two strategies: engineer microbes in such a way that they either live on cheaper substrates, or modify them so that they produce the more rare and expensive oils.[75] In both cases, the Third World loses out.

Interchanging products, markets and producers

The restructuring of the markets for sugar, cocoa and vegetable oils as described above are just a few examples of how biotechnology will affect the Third World as agricultural commodity exporters. There are many more. Vanilla, a crop on which some 70,000 small farmers in Madagascar depend, is another candidate for substitution by cell cultures in fermentation tanks. So are a whole series of other high-value plant-derived flavourings now produced by Third World farmers. Sudanese farmers selling gum arabic produced by *Acacia* trees face substitution of this highly valuable export commodity by starch-based counterparts. Kenyan farmers might lose their income obtained from the production of natural plant-derived pyrethrum –a widely used insecticide – as biotechnologists perfect cell culture and enzyme technology to produce the same substance in the factory.[76] Researchers from India put the total amount that Third World farmers will lose because of these substitution processes for five groups of crops at some $10 billion in the medium term.[77] For all crops, losses might come close to $20 billion, which is more than a quarter of the value of all agricultural commodities that the Third World is currently exporting.

But the implications of biotechnology go far beyond the crop by crop substitution efforts currently being carried out. The new technologies increase the interchangeability of the raw materials used for the end products. We have already seen how biotechnologically modified products from different plants can result in more or less the same end product. A product such as HFCS, which is already competing with sugar, is not only derived from maize, but in principle also from wheat, potatoes, manioc and other crops. A similar scenario looms for protein production. The production of protein for cattle feed on the base of soybeans is already being threatened by the so-called Single Cell Protein (SCP) production. SCP technology simply sets modified micro-organisms to work to make proteins in huge fermentation tanks. Scientists still have difficulties in making the process commercially viable, but Hoechst, ICI and the Soviet Union are currently investing huge amounts of money in the further development of this process. The USSR claims it will be self-sufficient in cattle feed in 1990; this would restructure the entire world protein market. But also fish-meal exports from developing countries, and tapioca production in Thailand are in danger of being replaced. The EEC imposed a reduction on Thailand's tapioca exports for cattle feed to Europe. Because of the risk of a 'grain war' with the USA, the EEC is reluctant to impose restrictions on imports of maize derivatives from the USA, yet it finds it easy to do so with a developing country like Thailand that has no bargaining power at all.

Using biotechnology, all these different sources of protein, starch and oil are increasingly becoming interchangeable. Biotechnology makes food production more and more like an assembly industry. Crops as such are no longer agricultural commodities, but their molecular components increasingly are. Rather than a global market for soybeans, palm-oil or cocoa, one has to start thinking of global markets for starch, proteins, oils and fats. The fishermen in Peru, the soybean producers in Brazil and the factories of ICI and Hoechst are now competing for the same protein market. Similarly sugar-cane workers in Cuba, potato producers in the Netherlands, maize producers everywhere, and the synthetic sweetener factories in the North, are all vying for the same sweetener market.

Interchangeability of products also means interchangeability of producers. Users of the raw materials can choose from a plethora of sources, depending on world market prices, domestic technological progress and political stability in the region from which the commodity is obtained. Overall, this results in a further decrease in world market prices for agricultural raw materials and in a weakening of the position of the suppliers of raw materials, often the developing countries.

One of the consequences of this chain of events is the virtual collapse of international agreements on agricultural commodities. While such agreements have always been difficult to reach, not least because of the different interests and stages of development within the Third World bloc, biotechnology now threatens to render a bad situation worse. The new technologies make it impossible to predict what will happen on the world market, and price guarantees to the Third World are untenable in this context. Different developing countries take different positions depending on the extent to which they can make use of the new technologies, resulting in a further deterioration of the Third World as a negotiating bloc.

Many public interest groups have rightly criticized over-reliance on export crops, such as those mentioned above, at the expense of food production, and opposed the export-led strategies promoted by the World Bank and IMF aimed at raising cash for debt repayments. The disastrous impact that emphasis on export crops in developing countries has on national and local food production and supply is widely known. The same is true for the horrendous work and living conditions endured by countless plantation labourers. Third World governments need to promote development strategies that lead towards increased food security. The sudden disappearance of entire export markets due to technological advances elsewhere in the world is not in the interest of the Third World or its people; it merely adds to their already immense problems.

Rapid product displacement from one region to another has always affected the poor at the very beginning of the production chain: the small farmers and the landless wage workers. The disastrous situation for the labourers employed in indigo production in Asia, after indigo was replaced by aniline dyes from Germany at the end of the 19th century, is one example of how product displacement affected the poor. The tremendous recession in whole regions of South America after rubber production was first transferred to Asia, and later shifted to synthetic rubber produced in the North, is another.

There is no indication that product displacements caused by biotechnology will have a less dramatic impact. Actually, the sugar crisis – in which the new biotechnologies played an important role – is already an example of the opposite. As quoted at the beginning of this chapter, the European Commission predicts disaster for developing countries, and OECD experts tend to agree. Serious thoughts on how to avoid such a tragedy are, however, difficult to find in the official circles. Preoccupied by a determination to stay ahead in the biotech race, industrialized countries advocate policies that will further eliminate the need for imports from the South, regardless of the implications for the poor and resourceless.

Notes and references

1. Commission of the European Communities, Document COM(86) 550 final/2, 1986. Quoted in FAO, 'Implications of New Biotechnologies for the International Undertaking', CPGR/89/9, Rome, January 1989, p. 8.

2. OECD, *Biotechnology: Economic and Wider Impacts*, OECD, Paris, 1989, p. 81.

3. FAO, *Trade Yearbook 1987*, FAO, Rome, 1988.

4. Belinda Coote, *The Hunger Crop*, Oxfam, London, 1987, pp. 20–3.

5. Ibid., p. 47.

6. Ibid., p. 66.

7. FAO, *Commodity Review and Outlook, 1987–88*, FAO, Rome, 1988, p. 25. See also Belinda Coote, 1987, op. cit., p. 30.

8. Quoted in F. Clairmore, J. Cavanagh, *Merchants of Drinks*, Third World Network, Penang, 1988, p. 167.

9. FAO, *Trade Yearbook 1988*, op. cit.

10. Belinda Coote, 1987, op. cit., p. 65.

11. FAO,*Commodity Review and Outlook 1987–88*, op. cit., p. 24.

12. Belinda Coote, 1987, op. cit., pp. 60–2.

13. R. G. Lewis, 'The Sour Taste of Sugar', in *Ceres*, No. 118, FAO, Rome. 1978 and 1985 figures from *Biotechnology Revolution and the Third World*, RIS, New Delhi, 1988, p. 209.

14. FAO, *Trade Yearbook 1987*, op. cit.; and Bijlman et al., *The International Dimension of Biotechnology in Agriculture*, University of Amsterdam, April 1986, p. 46.

15. Quoted in Clairmore and Cavanagh, 1988, op. cit., p. 168.

16. Belinda Coote, 1987, op. cit., p. 14.

17. OECD, 1989, op. cit., p. 86.

18. Hanne Svarstad, *Biotechnology and the International Division of Labour*, University of Oslo, December 1988, p. 127.

19. OECD, 1989, op. cit., p. 87.

20. A. Sasson, *Biotechnologies and Development*, UNESCO, Paris, 1988, p. 274.

21. Belinda Coote, 1987, op. cit., p. 73.

22. OECD, 1989, op. cit., p. 87.

23. Ibid., p. 86.

24. See, for example, RAFI Communiqué, 'Biotechnology and Natural Sweetners: Thaumatin', RAFI, Pittsboro, February 1987, for an excellent overview of research on thaumatin.

25. Tate & Lyle estimate. In *Derwent Biotechnology Abstracts*, Derwent Publications Limited, 1987, Entry No. 87–13068.

26. Sasson, 1987, op. cit., p. 270.

27. RAFI Communiqué. February 1987, op. cit. Price estimate from A. Sasson, 1988, op. cit.

28. Sasson, 1988, op. cit., p. 270.

29. Ibid.

30. Derwent, 1987, op. cit., Entry No. 87–13068.

31. Rein Dekker, 'Multinationals en de Internationale herstrukturering van de cacaosektor', in *Marquetalia*, No. 6, de Uitbuyt, Wageningen, 1983.

32. Ibid.

33. FAO, *FAO Agricultural Commodity Projections to 1990*, Rome, 1986, p. 123.

34. FAO, *Production Yearbook 1987*, Rome, 1988.

35. FAO, 1986, op. cit.; and FAO, *Commodity Review and Outlook 1987–1988*, Rome, 1988.

36. Transnational Information Exchange (TIE), 'Cocoa Processing and Chocolate Production' Conference report, TIE, Amsterdam, 1988, pp. 3–4.

37. FAO, *Commodity Review and Outlook*, 1988, op. cit., p. 29.

38. 'Bitter Times for Cocoa Growers', in *Business Week*, 4 April 1988, p. 37; and TIE, 1988, op. cit.

39. FAO, 1986, op. cit.

40. TIE, 1988, op. cit., p. 9.

41. In *Africa Research Bulletin*, Africa Research Limited, Vol. 26, 30 June 1989, p. 9583.

42. 'Bitter Times for Cocoa Growers', op. cit.

43. *Africa Research Bulletin*, Vol. 25, 30 April 1988, p. 9082.

44. *Africa Research Bulletin*, Vol. 26, 30 June 1989, p. 9583.

45. 'K. Guthrie To Continue Diversifying Crop Mix', in *Business Times*, 12 April 1988.

46. RAFI, 'Cacao & Biotechnology: A Report on Work in Progress', *RAFI Communiqué*, Pittsboro, May 1987, p. 3.

47. European Patent Office, Application No. 88106774.8, 27 April 1988.

48. Dekker, 1983, op. cit. Calculation based on UNCTAD data.

49. Quoted in Hanne Svarstad, 1988, op. cit., p. 169.

50. Ibid., p. 173.

51. *Derwent Biotechnology Abstracts*, Derwent Publications Limited, 1989, Entry No. 07054.

52. Hanne Svarstad, 1988, op. cit., p. 180.

53. Derwent, 1989, op. cit., Entry Nos. 89–02092 and 89-02093.

54. *RAFI Communiqué*, 1987, op. cit.

55. Derwent, 1989, op. cit., Entry No. 89–05195.

56. Hanna Svarstad, 1988, op. cit., p. 186.

57. FAO, *Agricultural Commodity Projections to 1990*, 1986, op. cit.

58. FAO, *Trade Yearbook 1987*, op. cit., figures for 1987.

59. FAO, *Agricultural Commodity Projections to 1990*, op. cit., (1990 figures is a FAO projection).

60. 'Biotechnologies des Corps Gras', in *Biofutur*, February 1986, p. 20.

61. 'Biotechnology and Vegetable Oils Focus on Oil Palm,' *RAFI Communiqué*, June 1988, Pittsboro.

62. Sasson, 1988, op. cit., pp. 25–31, 319–22.

63. Ibid., p. 28.

64. *RAFI Communiqué*, June 1988, op. cit., Figure cited is £ Sterling 17.5 million.

65. 'Sex Problem in the Plantations', in *South Magazine*, London, January 1987.

66. Sondahl et al., in *ATAS Bulletin*, UNCSTD, Vol. 1, No. 1, New York, 1984.

67. In *Far Eastern Economic Review*, 8 October 1987, p. 91.

68. FAO, *Production Yearbook 1987*, op. cit.

69. *RAFI Communiqué*, June 1988, op. cit.

70. Bijlman, v/d Doel, Junne, 'The Impact of Biotechnology on Living and Working Conditions in Western Europe and the Third World'. University of Amsterdam, Amsterdam, April 1986 (Doc. No. 85–1.3.5–3030–16).

71. Ibid.

72. Quotes from *In Search of Progress: Science, Technology and Unilever*, Unilever, Weert, The Netherlands, 1985, pp. 25, 28.

73. *Chemical & Engineering News*, 29 April 1985.

74. Interview with Geoffrey Allen of Unilever, in *Biofutur*, Paris, January 1988, pp. 20–2.

75. 'Biotechnologies des Corps Gras', in *Biofutur*, Paris, February 1986, p. 26.

76. For case studies on these examples, see C. Fowler et al., 'The Laws of Life', in *Development Dialogue*, Dag Hammarskjold Foundation, 1988, nr. 1–2.

77. V. R. Panchamukhi, N. Kumar, 'Impact on Commodity Exports', in *Biotechnology Revolution and the Third World*, RIS, New Delhi, 1988, p. 218.

7.   Controlling the Profit

'Patents are a paradise for parasites.'
'Patents protection forms a stumbling block for the development of trade and industry.'
'The patent system is a playground for plundering patent agents and lawyers.'
(J. Geigy-Merian, Geigy Firm – later Ciba-Geigy, 1883)[1]

'It is Ciba-Geigy's position that legal protection of intellectual property serves the public interest by stimulating continuing investment in technological innovation.'
(John H. Duesing, Ciba-Geigy, 1989)[2]

One century might seem a long time. It was certainly long enough for companies like Ciba-Geigy to change their minds about what to think of intellectual property systems. From describing patent systems as a paradise for parasites to considering them to be serving the public interest is quite a leap indeed. In the 19th century, Geigy and colleagues from other Swiss firms were in a vehement battle against any form of patent protection and had managed five times to reject calls for a national referendum on the matter. When two referenda on patent protection were finally held in 1882 and 1886, they were successfully defeated, largely due to the intense lobbying activities of Geigy and friends.

Now, over one hundred years later, Ciba-Geigy sends company representatives all over the globe to promote stronger patent protection for everything that can be made in its laboratories; and that includes life forms. With almost emotional arguments, companies now try to convince the world that there is no progress, no development and no happiness without strong intellectual property systems. Those countries which do not have them are charged with 'theft' and 'piracy', and accused of putting national interest above 'internationally accepted principles of fair trade'.[3]

An historical appraisal

If the only question then is to be fair, why this 180 degree shift in position within the same company over one century? The answer to this question is complex and can be answered only in its historical context. A hundred years ago, those in favour of free trade battled against those who pleaded for the granting of patent monopolies. Today, the lobby for stronger patent protection worldwide is aggressively waving the banner of free trade and bemoans the lack of intellectual property systems as a non-tariff barrier.

What is clear if one looks at the history of the patent debate is that the assumption that patent protection stimulates innovation is not as sound as today's promoters of the patent system would have us believe. The very reason for opposing strong patent protection a century ago by many Europeans and today by most Third World countries, lies in the conviction that the patent system does, in fact, exactly the opposite: blocking innovation and creating dependence. The crux underlying the different positions is whether you import or export technology. A hundred years ago, many European countries were technology importers, the NICs (Newly Industrializing Countries) of the late 19th century. Their nationally oriented industries vehemently opposed the idea of having to pay royalties for the products and processes they were using. The quotes from Geigy and friends at the beginning of this chapter speak for themselves.

The Third World NICs of today find themselves in a similar position. Of the 3.5 million patents in existence worldwide in the 1970s, only about 200,000 were granted by developing countries. The vast majority of these, some 84%, were owned by foreigners, especially by TNCs from the five richest countries.[4] Graph 7.1 looks at the situation in Asia and Latin America and confirms this biased functioning of the patent system, at least for developing countries. Most significant is that less than five per cent of these foreign-owned patents were actually used in production processes in the developing countries.[5] In a recent report (1988), the Inter-American Development Bank pointed out with concern that most foreign-owned patents in Latin American countries are never used there, but rather function to secure, protect or monopolize import flows.[6] A decade earlier, two United Nations Agencies – the World Intellectual Property Organization (WIPO) and the UN Conference on Trade and Development (UNCTAD) – had reached the same conclusion. In a joint study they affirmed:

> Instead of being used in production, an overwhelming majority of patents granted to foreigners through national laws of developing countries have been used to secure import monopolies.[7]

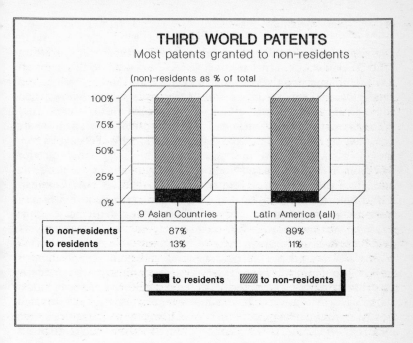

THIRD WORLD PATENTS
Most patents granted to non-residents

	9 Asian Countries	Latin America (all)
to non-residents	87%	89%
to residents	13%	11%

to residents ▓ to non-residents

In the 1960s it gradually became clear that prevailing intellectual property systems, rather than stimulating transfer of technology, were really functioning to transfer income from technology importers to exporters. The Third World started to react, and after a decade of negotiations in UNCTAD, strong and precise recommendations to revise the global intellectual property system resulted. Developing and developed countries agreed that such a revision should meet the special needs of the Third World in order to 'become more satisfactory instruments for aiding developing countries in the transfer and development of technology.'[8] Meanwhile, developing countries began to change their national laws, excluding certain products from patent protection, strengthening provisions for compulsory licensing, and limiting the duration of patents.[9] In 1975, WIPO member states began negotiating the revision at the Paris Convention which governs patent law at the international level.

The great reversal

But then came what Surendra Patel, former UNCTAD official deeply involved in the patent debate, calls 'The Great Reversal'.[10] While in the 1960s and beginning of the 1970s calls for a New International Economic Order echoed loudly in the corridors and meeting rooms of the United Nations, the late 1970s and 1980s witnessed a mounting economic crisis and the rise of 'no-nonsense' and protectionist attitudes in the North. In 1974, the OECD Council still warned member states, in unusually strong language, against 'abusive practices in which patentee and their licensees may engage'.[11] One decade later, the same OECD countries pushed the discussions to the Uruguay Round of the General Agreement on Tariffs and Trade (GATT) where the dissident voices of the Third World are hardly heard. After having effectively blocked the UNCTAD and WIPO negotiations, the North is now ruthlessly pushing ahead for universal patent protection, based on their own laws and traditions. In the discussions on Trade Related Aspects of Intellectual Property Rights (TRIPS) of GATT, even the initial ministerial declaration of the GATT Uruguay Round, in which the industrialized countries explicitly promised not to push for measures that might be inconsistent with the need of developing ones,[12] seems to have been forgotten.

Discussions on the special needs of developing countries and about the importance of using the patent system as an instrument for national development and technology transfer, have been substituted by simple arguments that the North is losing huge amounts of money because the South does not have strong patent protection. The US Chemical Manufacturers Association (CMA) reports US chemical industry losses of up to $6 billion annually due to intellectual property infringements. PMA, their pharmaceutical counterpart, claims they are losing $4 billion a year to 'intellectual property piracy'.[13] The US International Trade Commission (US-ITC) circulates estimates from a low $43 billion to a high $102 billion for American business alone,[14] while the International Chamber of Commerce puts the losses at $70 billion worldwide.[15] These extravagant claims by industry, though mostly unsubstantiated, are repeated by the US government to increase the patent pressure on developing and other countries.[16]

The figures are completely out of touch with reality. If the US-ITC claims were to be extrapolated to other OECD countries, we would be talking about anything between $100 and $300 billion in 'lost' income from the South. This compares with total Third World exports of some $500 billion in 1987.[17] In practice, this means that industrialized countries, through strengthened patent systems in the South, are requesting enormous amounts of additional revenue to be transferred from the South to the North. It would make the net South-North transfer of funds, currently in the order of $50 billion a year, crippling as it already is, seem insignificant. This 'scare-the-hell-out-of-you' strategy is absurd and constrasts sharply with the more serious attempts to analyse and revise the patent system also to benefit Third World development, undertaken at UNCTAD a decade earlier.

The USA is not waiting for the outcome of the GATT Uruguay Round to settle its grievances. Bilaterally, it has already started to sanction those developing countries without strong patent regimes. In 1988, the Reagan administration passed a new Trade Act, which includes the setting-up of a watch list of infringing countries. A study has already been drawn up on 36 countries, including Brazil, China, India, Korea, Mexico, Taiwan and Thailand, all of which are now under strong pressure to amend their patent laws. If the countries fail to respond in a way that pleases the USA, trade sanctions will follow. Several countries can already explain what that means. In late 1988, the Reagan administration increased import tariffs on $165 million worth of goods from Thailand because of lax enforcements of intellectual property laws in that country.[18] Also in 1988, Brazil faced similar retaliations, when the US imposed punitive tariffs, valued at $39 million, on Brazilian imports to the US because that country does not allow for patents on pharmaceutical products.[19] Some countries have started giving in to the pressure by changing their laws, but many are resisting. The stakes are simply too high.

The bitter irony of this bully-strategy lies in its double standards. On the one hand, the OECD is requesting Third World countries to strengthen their patent laws in order to allow TNCs from the North to monopolize markets in the South. But on the other hand, the same OECD countries carefully protect their own markets from imports from the South with a whole arsenal of measures including subsidies, quotas and tariffs. It is estimated that in the United States alone this protection covered 25% of all US imports in 1986, compared to 8% in 1975.[20] The situation in Europe and Japan is hardly different. At the same time, since 1980 the US Congress has quietly passed 13 laws on intellectual property protection to make the American bully-strategy more operational. Even basic science suffers. In 1987 the Reagan administration ordered that US agencies sign scientific research agreements only with those countries that respect US patents. According to the magazine *Trends in Biotechnology*, the new laws considerably favour US nationals in the application for patents.[21] One of these laws, for example, rules that US patents are granted to residents from other countries only if those countries have brought their patent protection in line with US standards.[22] This 'patent nationalism' is exactly the basis on which the US accuses other countries of unfair practices.

The second irony lies in the patent history of countries such as Japan and the USA. Japan has joined the USA in the current GATT negotiations in trying to push stronger patent protection into the Third World. Until not so long ago, Japan itself was a newly industrializing country that, according to many observers, developed on the basis of imitation. Now Japan is among the countries that want to close this route for others. In the 19th century the USA itself was attacked by Britain, then world leader in technology, for not providing strong patent protection. The *Washington Post* reported that these complaints had little effect; American companies wanted the freedom to capitalize quickly on British innovations.[23]

The battle over whether pharmaceutical products should be patented is a good example of the biased arguments of the North. Many Third World countries do not allow patenting on drugs because they regard secure indigenous capacities in this field as vital for national development. Some, like Brazil, have already been punished for that. But major OECD countries themselves started allowing for product patents on drugs only after their pharmaceutical industries had become firmly established: France in 1958, West Germany in 1968, and Switzerland in 1977. The Japanese only allowed for pharmaceutical product patents in 1976 when their country already ranked second in world production in drugs, and controlled 80% of its home market.[24] These figures might lead to the conclusion that the national pharmaceutical sector in many OECD countries was able to grow precisely because of the convenient absence of strong domestic patent protection for drugs. Only when export interests began to dominate did patent protection appear more desirable. The North, through its demands in GATT, is now seeking to deny the Third World that same route to development. This new technological protectionism would result in the perpetuation of current comparative advantages of the industrialized countries in world production and trade.[25] It would also further warp the existing international division of labour, already heavily biased towards the interest of the North.

In discussions on development, experts from the North often quickly point to the Asian NICs, such as Singapore, Hong Kong and the Republic of Korea, as extremely successful development models that should also be followed by other Third World countries. Yet, again, much of the economic success there was based on freely using and building upon knowledge and technology from the North. Korea and others are now on the US patent watch list. Ultimately, the issue boils down to the question of whether or not sovereign nations, especially those from the Third World, have the right to choose the policy instruments that most suit their national development needs. Perhaps the time has come to start arguing for the Right to Imitate, rather than the Right to Intellectual Property. Historical evidence might show that much of the economic and industrial advancement of OECD countries has been based on exactly that.

Tightening the grip: the push for patents on life

Imitation is precisely one of the main problems for the emerging biotechnology industries. The raw material of biotechnology – genetic resources – tends to imitate itself continuously, and without human intervention. During the heated discussions on intellectual property protection towards the end of the last century, the question of how to apply such protection to living matter was hardly considered. The reproductive forces of life were considered too unpredictable even to start trying to make money on them. But that began to change as the bio-sciences developed to a stage where, through systematic research, life forms could be changed and brought to the market place. After the work of Gregor Mendel and the rediscovery of his laws of inheritance at the beginning of this century, systematic plant-breeding started to take off. With plant-breeding maturing into an industrial activity, pressure to protect the ownership of the resulting products grew. But 'life' never fitted comfortably into the rigid industrial patent schemes. Seeds change, mutate and reproduce – all too difficult for patent systems, which were designed for inanimate products of manufacture.

The political problems are, however, even greater than the technical ones. As late as the 1960s, when preparing the European Patent Convention, the Europeans were still involved in a heated debate on whether food, chemicals, plants and animals should be included in the patent regime. The debate was not so much on technicalities, but much more on the question as to whether society should grant monopoly rights in these fundamental sectors. They decided that plants and animals should stay outside the industrial patent system and adopted a special protection regime for plants: the Plant Breeders' Rights system (PBR). In 1961 the Union for the Protection of New Varieties of Plants (UPOV) was formed, and the UPOV Convention was signed by a number of – mainly European – industrialized states.

In the 1970s the USA and several other industrialized countries joined the UPOV Convention, but the growth of UPOV came to a halt by the end of the 1970s when several industrial states did not ratify the Convention and efforts to persuade the developing countries to join the club backfired. A major reason for this setback was increased recognition of the negative impact of PBR for plant breeding. Evidence began to appear that because of PBR, multinational companies started to take control of the breeding sector. It was also argued that the PBR system, because of its requirements of uniformity, promotes a further impoverishment of genetic diversity and that it hardly contributes to the development of new qualitatively distinct varieties. Developing countries recognized that PBR would not favour the build-up of strong national agricultural systems, but on the contrary would jeopardize efforts to establish an independent national breeding sector.[26] The UPOV Convention has attracted only 19 member states up to now, and with the industrial patent system moving in its future looks bleak.

A major difference between the Plant Breeders' Rights and industrial patent systems lies in the scope of protection granted. PBR gives the breeder, for a certain period of time, exclusive monopoly control on the reproduction of a plant variety for commercial purposes, its marketing and sale. Under the current UPOV Convention, the protected plant variety can be freely used by others for further breeding and by farmers for repeated planting. PBR does not provide ownership over the germplasm in the seed, it gives only a monopoly right for the selling and marketing of a specific variety.

The monopoly rights of industrial patents go much further. With the PBR system, the protection is always limited to a specific plant variety. A patent, however, can be claimed on virtually anything: from a specific DNA sequence to a whole set of plants and animals, and everything in between. The only conditions are that what you claim must be new, it must involve an 'inventive' (non-obvious) step, and it must be useful for something. It is up to the patent office to decide whether these rules of the patent game have been met.

The extension of the industrial patent system to living matter carried an incredible number of problems. Some of these lie in the characteristics of the patent system itself. One of the requirements for a valid patent is that the item to be protected must be a new invention, not a discovery, and it must be non-obvious. But where is the borderline in biology? 'Who will have the guts to declare a gene novel and non-obvious? Would anyone know enough of genetics and nature to claim such arrogance?' cried a desperate plant-breeder at a recent conference on life patents.[27] His frustration is quite understandable. Plant-breeders have, through cross-breeding, moved genetic material around for many years. Farmers have done it for thousands of years. Nature has done it from the very beginning! Now biotechnologists are claiming intellectual property on isolated and cloned genes, cells and entire living beings. Who, then, decides what is new, what is non-obvious?

Another problem is linked to the 'exhaustion principle' of current patent laws. It holds that the monopoly ends once the product is brought to the market. No patent law prevents me from buying a television set and then using it as a fish tank; or from selling it to someone else. But the exhaustion principle makes life difficult for those who want to patent engineered living matter, as this tends to reproduce itself, making unlimited free copies of the patented material. They do not want to see their patent exhausted at the moment the farmer puts seed in the soil.

The patent system, then, would have to be reconstructed to cope with life forms. In practice, however, patent lawyers are doing just the opposite: redefining biology to fit patent law. This is when the most eloquent arguments start. Several centuries ago, Linneaus came up with classifications to create some order in the human mind with respect to the natural 'chaos' out there. Patent examiners today need different classifications to decide on what is patentable. The results are often outrageous as a recent EEC biotechnology patent proposal shows. This text defines a cell as a microorganism,[28] which prompted members of the European Parliament to joke about elephants consisting of an immense heap of microbes. For the European patent lawyers the logic is simple: micro-organisms are patentable, and if individual cells are included in the same group, they become patentable as well. On the other hand, the European Patent Office points out that the new definition of a plant variety proposed by UPOV,[29] would include items such as individual cells, protoplasts, DNA itself and even 'all green plants'.[30] According to the European Commission, a cell is a microorganism; according to UPOV, a cell is a plant variety. Are we to conclude then that a plant variety is a micro-organism?!

Debate in the international community on the patenting of plants, animals, genes and processes has only just begun. The push for strong patents comes, of course, from the major corporations that are now investing heavily in biotechnology. The problem for the proponents is that existing legal conventions would have to be changed to make all their wishes come true. This is especially the case in Europe. The European Patent Convention (EPC), signed by 13 European countries and adopted as late as 1973, specifically excludes 'plant or animal varieties or essentially biological processes for the production of plants and animals' from patentability.[31] As was made abundantly clear in the documents of the Council of Europe when member states were laying the groundwork for this Convention in the 1960s, these exclusions were meant to apply to animals and plants in general, and were incorporated because 'they derive largely from considerations of public interest'.[32] For the same reasons, pharmaceuticals and food products were put forward for exclusion but these exceptions were scrapped during the negotiations despite strong opposition, especially from Austria.[33]

Policy makers are known to be short of historical memory. For the officials at the European Commission, 'the public interest' must be something that mutates rapidly and depends largely on the interests of the industry. In 1988, only 15 years after the adoption of the EPC, the European Commission published a draft law proposal ('directive') on the patenting of biotechnological inventions.[34] At this time of writing, the directive is under heated negotiation at different levels. If adopted, it would make everything from a gene to entire classes of living beings patentable in the European Community. To avoid open clashes with the European Patent and the UPOV Conventions, the directive excludes plant and animal varieties and essentially biological processes from patentability, but redefines those terms in such a way that virtually the entire plant and animal kingdoms are up for intellectual property protection. In the EEC proposal, everything is patentable, as long as you do not call it a 'variety'. Even human beings are not specifically excluded. Rather than going through the long and tedious process of renegotiating international conventions such as the EPC, the Commission is proposing simply to redefine their basic assumptions. The European Patent Office itself is not very happy with such manoeuvres. It has publicly stated to the European Commission that if the aim is to make plants and animals patentable, then 'the right approach would be to revise the EPC itself'.[35]

The legal situation in the United States is more open to plant and animal patenting due to the historical particularity of this country. After two important legal decisions, one by the US Supreme Court in the Chakrabarty case (1980) and one by the US Board of Patent Appeals in the Hibberd case (1985), industrial patent protection can now be granted to plants. It is expected that a major shift will now take place in the US from PBR to industrial patents.[36] Once seeds were eligible for industrial patents in the US, it was not long before the first animal patent was granted. On 12 April 1988, this dubious honour fell to a little mouse into which a human cancer gene was grafted. The applicant was Harvard University, but the monopoly went to Du Pont, the multinational company who paid for the research.

The implications

When experts squabble over legal mechanisms, the real implications of life patents are often muddled and lost. A patent is, after all, a concession by society to a private inventor. A monopoly is granted in return for perceived advantages to society. So what does society get in return? 'Innovation!' some point out quickly. 'Technological progress!' others cry. The assumptions are plentiful and bold, but the hard empirical data supporting them difficult to find. In a press release presenting the EEC patent directive, the Commission points with a sense of panic to the position of biotech competitors in the United States and Japan, and warns that Europe should not stay behind.[37] On the other side of the Atlantic Ocean, North American citizens are told that the Europeans and Japanese are closing in quickly in the field of biotechnology, and that the US needs further to strengthen its patent laws. It seems that the 'biotech-race' itself forms sufficient justification to extend monopoly patents to life. But when one goes beyond the logic of such blind, competitive rhetorics, and takes a closer look at what life patents really mean for society, the emerging picture is not as positive as the patent-pushers might want us to believe. In Box 7.1 an overview of possible implications is reproduced. Without trying to be complete or exhaustive, the 'twelve reasons' do give considerable food for thought.

In late 1987, top officials of the US biotechnology company Genetics Institute Inc. gathered at their headquarters to settle an important issue: which version of a new clot-dissolving drug to invest in. With money to develop just one of the four potential products, the company's scientists argued for the one that had the most positive research results. Then the attorneys weighed in. They pushed a drug that had not tested as well, but would command the broadest patent. And they won hands down. 'Researchers used to be up in arms if such crass decisions were made', says the company's patent counsel Bruce M. Eisen. But now 'the strength of the potential patent position is a leading factor in what research to pursue'.[38]

This ominous example from the pharmaceutical sector could have been taken from any other. Rather than simply stimulating innovation, the patent system applied to living matter redirects attention towards those products that provide for the broadest and easiest patent protection. Rather than

Twelve Reasons to say no to life patents

If the patenting of life forms is accepted...

1. FARMERS will be obliged to pay royalties on every generation of plants and livestock they buy and reproduce for production purposes. Prices for patented genetically engineered 'miracle' seeds and breeds will be far higher than traditional strains and it will be illegal for farmers and herders to biologically renew their stock without permission or payment. Thus, the rural community will lose its last thread of control over the first link in the food chain and become totally dependent on multinational corporations.

2. BREEDERS will no longer have free access to germplasm for developing new varieties of plants and animals. Genetic resources, including genes, cell lines, protoplasts and even characteristics (like 'high yield'), will become the exclusive property of top biotechnology firms. Licences will have to be obtained and royalties paid for, in order for breeders to be able to incorporate patented genes and characteristics into new crop and animal varieties. Most independent breeders will simply go out of business. As a result, the only innovation in the breeding sector will be found in the legal departments of large corporations where patent lawyers will dictate the direction of biological research.

3. CONSUMERS are likely to end up paying higher prices for food, medicine and other products of biotechnology. In buying patented genetically engineered products, consumers will be unwittingly subsidising industry as royalty charges will be passed on to the end product. For example, a new brand of biotechnologically produced beer could be patented first for the strain of barley used, secondly for the fermentation procedure and thirdly for its processing technique! Additionally, the type of new foods the consumer can choose from will be determined more by the patentability of its components than by its quality.

4. PUBLIC RESEARCH will be undermined and effectively privatised. The public sector is paid for by all of us, but the extension of the patent system will ensure that only private industry benefits. Universities and public research institutes will be obliged to keep secret their research results funded by the private sector, while the corporations apply for their patents. This means that the public exposure and circulation of scientific information will be restricted drastically, to the detriment of learning and innovation.

5. MARKET STRUCTURES will undergo a dramatic wave of increased concentration. Fewer firms will be able to compete on the market place and many will be bought out by the strongest multinational corporations. Stronger monopoly structures in the agribusiness, pharmaceutical and chemical sectors will emerge, with their consequences on prices and quality, leaving us few choices in our needs for food, health and a cleaner environment.

6. GENETIC DIVERSITY will suffer tremendous erosion as monopoly control over genetic resources severely restricts their circulation and destroys their status as The Common Heritage of Mankind. Without our wealth of genetic resources, food and medicinal production systems cannot cope with constantly evolving social and ecological pressures. If those resources become the exclusive property of a few corporations, genetic uniformity will increase substantially and society will have to pay the bill.

7. FOOD SUPPLY will be threatened by monopoly control over genetic resources, farmers' harvests and the processed results. Patent holders will have more power to decide what we eat. Such excessive control over the food supply is extremely dangerous as just a few integrated firms will dominate the sector. Also, public measures to control and direct agricultural production will be jeopardised, as patent priorities take over from common sense. Life patents will move research in biotechnology further away from public institutions and thus from public influence over whether, how and for whom it should be developed.

8. THE THIRD WORLD will increasingly lose access to scientific information and technology transfer, and will see their freely donated biological resources privatised by the North. Patenting life would also mean a total denial of farmers' rights in the South to compensation for all the work they do in providing the world economy with rich and useful genetic diversity. With the current proposal, the only forms of human innovation that will not be patentable will be those of farmers and communities in the Third World. The developing countries will also have to pay higher prices for patented inventions, thus aggravating debt burdens and the marginalisation of the poor.

9. The whole concept of **HUMAN RIGHTS** will be undermined, as human beings and parts of their body can become the exclusive property of patent holders. That corporations can own your organs, physical traits or intimate genetic information is a total denial of the individual's right to an independent existence and to control over his/her very body. It will also exacerbate organ-trafficking and eugenic tendencies in medicine.

10. ANIMAL WELFARE will become a nostalgic notion of the past, as patenting stimulates the genetic engineering of animals to suffer as they serve industrial systems for the production of food and medicine. Patented farm animals will be victims of severe stress, their bodies designed to produce leaner meat, higher milk yield and an assortment of pharmaceutical products. The 'Harvard mouse', which was patented in the USA to produce breast cancer, is the very first of a whole range of animals that will be genetically transformed and patented for the sole purpose of suffering as models of human diseases.

11. SOCIETY'S RELATIONSHIP TO NATURE will be reduced to a commercial enterprise based on exploitation and profit. Patenting life means that some people can intellectually own the very foundations of living matter and life cycles, thereby undermining any last thread of respect for nature in our already artificialised world. Biotechnology 'inventors' do not create nature, they simply cut it into pieces and claim ownership over it. Such arrogance towards the world around us has already done tremendous damage and is a suicidal attitude towards the system that sustains us.

12. ETHICAL & RELIGIOUS VALUES based on respect for life, creation and reproduction will be thoroughly subverted. The patenting of genetic materials forces upon us a reductionistic and materialistic concept of life as a mere collection of chemical substances that happen to be able to reproduce and can be manipulated and owned.

Source: This box was adapted from '12 reasons for 12 EEC member states to say: no to patents on life', GRAIN, Barcelona, 1990.

promoting competition in research and development, it limits the involvement to those who can afford to pay for the royalties or have other patents to offer in exchange.

In the field of agriculture, the patenting of plants and animals and their genetic materials would make it impossible for breeders freely to use each others' breeding material. Using a plant or animal with something patented in it to breed something better would then require permission from and payment to the patentee. In plant and animal breeding, the unrestricted use of existing varieties and races for further improvement forms the very backbone of the whole sector. Abolishing this practice by the introduction of industrial patent systems would mean quite simply the destruction of what is left of the independent plant-breeding industry. It would also effectively bring animal-breeding, currently in many countries still under control of farmers or the state, under control of large TNCs.

Jack Kloppenburg, in his study on the transformation of the seeds industry, gives a striking example of the early patenting days in the United States.[39] By the end of the 1950s, hybrid maize had been available to US farmers for more than two decades. A major problem for the breeders offering hybrid maize was the fact that the inbred lines used for the production of the hybrids had to be de-tasselled manually to avoid self-pollination. This delicate manual operation involved the training, organizing, supervising and paying of some 125,000 labourers each summer, costing the seed companies an estimated $10 million annually. D. F. Jones, a plant-breeder working in the public sector, had been pioneering the production of hybrid maize. He developed a technique to produce 'cytoplasmic male sterility' (CMS), which eliminated this painstaking and costly manual process. This technique incorporates genetic factors in the maize that make the male parent lines sterile, thus avoiding self-pollination and the need for de-tasselling.

Jones, unusually for public sector breeders at the time, took out a patent on this revolutionary technique and assigned it to the public institution he was working with. The private seed industry did not take long to adopt this technology, but refused to pay royalties to the public sector. Only after being forced by litigation several years later, in 1969, did the companies start paying royalties. Although the use of CMS lines reduced the de-tasselling cost for seed companies by as much as a factor of 25, the price of hybrid maize seed increased by over six per cent from 1958, when companies started using the male sterility process commercially, to 1965, when the process was ubiquitous. DeKalb, now a giant in the US maize-breeding industry, promised that, 'If everyone stops detasseling, and passes all the benefit on to the consumer by lower prices, then the farmer is the only one who gains.' The opposite proved to be true.

The male sterility story would probably have developed quite differently had it taken place in the 1990s. Firstly, it is most likely that the technique would have been developed by the private sector itself. The bulk of current hybrid maize technology in North America is staunchly controlled by a few multinational companies. Pioneer, DeKalb/Pfizer, Ciba-Geigy, Sandoz and Upjohn together govern over two-thirds of the US maize seed market.[40] Even if it had been developed at a US university, it is likely that it would have used funds from private industry with the corporation retaining the property rights. Secondly, the company in question would not only have patented the process, as Jones did, but also the genes involved, the cells and all maize plants and products derived from it. Thirdly, it is likely that the company would not have limited its patent claim to maize only, but to any plant into which the new process and genes could be incorporated. And lastly, and perhaps most importantly, the company might choose not to license the technology to other breeders, but to retain exclusive use for its own varieties. With such a crucial technique as male sterility, which has been incorporated into virtually every maize plant, this would extend one company's control to dominate the entire maize seed market.

Another feature of the patent system is that it allows for multiple patents as well as for multiple claims within a patent to be made on a single product. In the end we will be in a situation where a single plant, animal or microbe contains many different patented parts. What this can mean for an average plant-breeder might be illustrated with the following example:

> Sometime in the near future Dr Smith, a well-respected plant breeder, wants to cross an existing widely used variety of maize, 'Higrow', with another, 'Reliant', in order to produce a new variety that incorporates a useful resistance from 'Reliant' into 'Higrow'. First he has to find out whether there are any patented genes, cells or other genetic information in the two varieties. He discovers that 'Higrow' contains patented materials from six different chemical companies, while 'Reliant' has three patented genes in it. Further, he finds out that three special techniques he planned to use for the crossing are also patented. Before Dr Smith – used to doing his work without restrictions – can get his new variety to the market, he has to seek permission from nine companies and pay them royalties, and additionally negotiate with three other companies to use the breeding techniques. Dr Smith, along with many of his colleagues, will probably decide to drop out of business and look for another job. If, however, he manages to get the required permissions and pay all the royalties involved, he will have to raise the price of his new variety considerably in order to recoup some of the costs. So not only Dr Smith, but also the farmers – and in the end the consumers – lose out.[41]

Before deciding to sell out, Dr Smith might encounter a few other problems resulting from life patents. A carefully drawn-up patent can claim intellectual property on characteristics independent from the genetic material itself. US Patent No. 4,581,847 is for cereals with a high content of a specific protein: tryptophane. The patent document explains that' . . .mutant plants have an endogenous free tryptophane content of at least ten times the amount of corresponding non mutant . . . plants' fall within the scope of the invention,[42] irrespective of the genes that code for it. If Dr Smith happens to be in the business of breeding cereals with a high content of this protein, he is well advised to ask the patentee in question to continue; this whole field of work might already be the property of the patentee. As UPOV pointed out in one of its documents,[43] such broadly defined patents could cover a whole range of already existing or still to be produced crop varieties, and can block entire fields of work in the breeding sector. This reportedly has already happened to sun-flower breeders in the USA, who received notice from one company, Sungene, that they had better stop working on sun-flower varieties with high oleic acid content. Sungene had obtained a US patent for this characteristic, and considered anyone else working on it as infringing the patent.[44] In 1990, the patent was revoked, but not before having 'effectively stopped' research on high oleic acid content in sun-flowers anywhere outside the company's laboratory.[45]

Apart from increasing the cost of the seed, the patent system extended to life forms penalizes the farmer in other ways. When using seed containing patented genetic material, it would be illegal for farmers freely to use part of the harvest for next year's sowing, as the germplasm in the seeds would continue to be owned by the patentee. The farmer would thus have to return to the market each year to purchase seed, as is now the case with hybrid crops. This would virtually eliminate a farming practice that is widespread in developing and developed countries – that of using saved seed for planting the following season. According to industry analysts, over a third of all seeds planted worldwide are supplied in this way,[46] and other estimates give much higher percentages of home-grown seed. Graph 7.2 shows the extent to which European farmers use certified seed for small grains. Most of the non-certified seed is home-grown. Graph 7.3 shows the extent to which US farmers use home-grown seed for specific crops. While use of such seed in the US and Europe is substantial, especially for non-hybrid crops, the use of home-grown seeds in developing countries is far greater.

The elimination of the use of home-grown seed would dramatically increase the farming community's dependence on the plant-breeding and biotechnology industries. It would also mean a prodigious loss of genetic diversity that is maintained in the field by farmers through the selection and use of their own seed. Finally, the costs to the farmer would be considerably increased. William Lesser, professor at Cornell University, estimated that a complete prohibition of farmer-saved seeds would cost American farmers over $500 million annually for soybean, wheat and cotton alone.[47] The same expert calculates that for British wheat and barley grow-

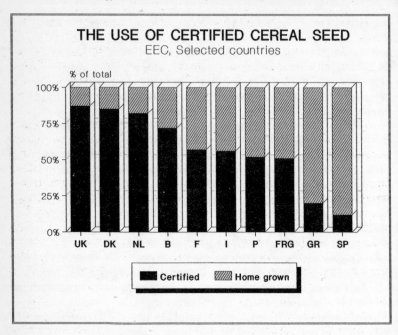

THE USE OF CERTIFIED CEREAL SEED
EEC, Selected countries

% of total

100%
75%
50%
25%
0%

UK DK NL B F I P FRG GR SP

■ Certified   ▨ Home grown

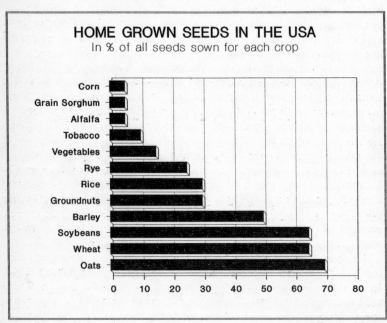

HOME GROWN SEEDS IN THE USA
In % of all seeds sown for each crop

Corn
Grain Sorghum
Alfalfa
Tobacco
Vegetables
Rye
Rice
Groundnuts
Barley
Soybeans
Wheat
Oats

0 10 20 30 40 50 60 70 80

ers these costs would be up to $80 million,[48] a figure that would be considerably higher for other European countries where home-grown seed is more commonly used. In the hypothetical case that home-grown seeds would be eliminated worldwide, farmers would end up paying an extra $6 billion annually![49] But Lesser's message is simple enough: 'Farmers, though, must overcome a psychological resistance to having the uses of their crops dictated by the legal system.'[50]

While the implications for crop growers are tremendous, those involved in raising animals might be even more seriously affected. In many countries genetic improvement of cattle is largely dominated by farmers and their co-operatives, and supported by public institutions. On many dairy farms, artificial insemination is combined with on-farm breeding using outstanding bulls raised by the farmers themselves. This practice has resulted in immense increases in the production of meat and milk, to the extent that most industrialized countries now produce surpluses. The biotechnology industry is now throwing its weight behind this system and will end up patenting the results. Dairy farmers will have to be careful when they inseminate their cattle with sperm containing patented genes. If a bull, resulting from such an insemination, runs around doing his biological duty, the farmer might find himself in court.

There are people who argue that life patents will especially help small breeding and biotech companies to survive. But a look at who applies for biotech patents might put such claims in context. A survey of patent applications to the European Patent Office up to April 1989 revealed 147 applications for plant-related patents.[51] Graph 7.4 shows the result if the applications are ordered by company. A full one-third of all applications come from just three large corporations: Lubrizol, Monsanto and Ciba-Geigy. All TNCs together are responsible for 56% of the applications. The TNCs, together with five major biotech companies, most of them heavily involved in contract research for TNCs, control almost three-quarters of all applications. The picture overall is that the patent system is by and large biased towards large corporations.

Ordered by country, the same data undermine one of the main arguments of the European Commission in pushing for strong patent protection. The Commission claims that life patents are the key to Europe's competitive advantage over the US industry. The US industry itself is, however, by far the largest applicant for European plant biotech patents. A strong European patent system is by no means a guarantee that the Europeans will profit most from it. It might just as well be the other way around.

If society allows for the industrial patent system to be applied to life forms, a turbulent 100 year history will have come to an unfortunate end. In 1883, a handful of industrialized countries, bringing along a few of their colonies, signed the Paris Convention in the midst of a debate in which many industrialists considered the patent system as a paradise for parasites.

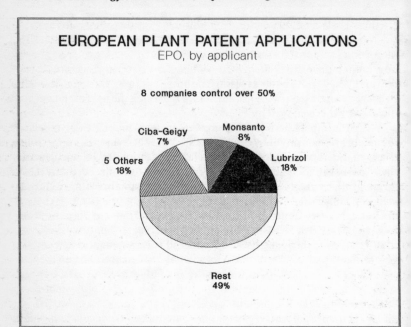

EUROPEAN PLANT PATENT APPLICATIONS
EPO, by applicant

8 companies control over 50%

Ciba-Geigy 7%
Monsanto 8%
Lubrizol 18%
5 Others 18%
Rest 49%

Those afraid of parasites were tranquillized with a whole series of concessions. Compulsory licensing would form a guarantee against abuse, and vital sectors such as food, chemicals and pharmaceuticals would be excluded. Living matter was not even under discussion. A century later, the roles are reversed. The parasites are now those who fail to provide for patent protection on everything. Plants, animals and humans are, with exceptions, the last survivors outside the monopoly system. Once they have been included, the circle will be complete.

Notes and references

1. J. Geigy-Merian et al., *Ein Beitrag zur Frage der Einführung des Patentschützes in der Schweitz*, Switzerland, 1883. (Geigy-Merian co-authored this publication with 10 other Swiss industrialists.)

2. J. Duesing, 'Patent Protection for Inventions from Agricultural Biotechnology', in 'Patenting Life Forms in Europe', Conference Proceedings, ICDA Seeds Campaign, Barcelona, 1989.

3. W. H. Duffey, 'Intellectual Property Needs of Multinationals', in 'Equitable Patent Protection for the Developing World', Cornell University Staff Paper 89–36, Ithaca, USA, November 1989.

4. UNCTAD/WIPO, *The Role of the Patent System in the Transfer of Technology to Developing Countries*, UN, New York, 1975.

5. Ibid.

6. Banco Interamericano de Desarrollo, *Progreso Economico y Social en America Latina: Informe 1988*, BID, Washington DC, 1988, p. 329.

7. UNCTAD/WIPO, 1975, op. cit.

8. Resolution adopted by Committee of Transfer of Technology of UNCTAD. 14th Meeting, 5 December 1975, UNCTAD, Geneva.

9. John Barton, 'Legal Trends and Agricultural Biotechnology: Effects on Developing Countries', in *Trends in Biotechnology*, Vol. 7, October 1989.

10. Surendra Patel, 'Intellectual Property Rights in the Uruguay Round', in *Economic and Political Weekly*, New Delhi, 6 May 1989, pp. 978–93.

11. OECD Council, 22 January 1974, quoted in Patel, 1989, op. cit.

12. Ministerial declaration on the Uruguay Round, Paragraph (v) of section B, as quoted in Patel, 1989, op. cit.

13. W. H. Duffey, 1989, op. cit.

14. US-ITC Report. Figures published in *Bioteknologi, Patenter: Et Internasjonalt Persecktiv*, Newsletter No. 1/2, 1989. Norwegian NIEO Group, Oslo, 1989.

15. Quoted in Patel, 1989, op. cit.

16. The US-ITC figures, for example, were given to the Norwegian embassy in Washington by US government officials. The USA considers Norwegian patent laws too weak, especially on pharmaceuticals.

17. UNCTAD, *Commodity Yearbook 1989*, UN, New York, 1989.

18. 'The Battle Raging over Intellectual Property', in *Business Week*, 22 May 1989.

19. 'Brazil says US Sanctions Breach Standstill Deal', in *Financial Times*, 28 October 1988.

20. P. R. De Almeida, 'The New Intellectual Property Regime', paper presented to the conference 'The Uruguay Round of GATT', Bergamo, 21–23 September 1989.

21. Arthur G. Cook, 'Patents as non-tariff trade barriers', in *Trends in Biotechnology*, Vol. 7, October 1989.

22. 'Fighting Trespassing on Intellectual Property', *Washington Post*, 6 December 1987. Quoted in *Bioteknologi, Patenter, Internasjonalt Perspectiv*, 1989, op. cit.

23. 'Fighting Trespassing on Intellectual Property', op. cit.

24. Sistema Economico Latinoamericano, 'Capitulos de SELA', SELA, Caracas, October/December, Caracas, 1988.

25. P. R. De Almeida, 1989, op. cit.

26. See, for example, Pat Mooney, 'The Law of the Seed', in *Development Dialogue*, No. 1–2, Uppsala, 1983.

27. J. G. Boonman, 'Plant Patenting as seen by a Plant Breeding Professional' in 'Patenting Life forms in Europe', Conference Proceedings, ICDA Seeds Campaign, Barcelona 1989.

28. Draft EEC Council Directive on the legal protection of Biotechnological inventions. EEC Doc. Com (88)–496, Brussels 1988.

29. 'Any plant or part of plant or any grouping of plants or parts of plants, which, by reason of its characteristics, is regarded as an independent unit for the purposes of cultivation or any other form of use'.

30. EPO, Standing Advisory Committee before the European Patent Office, 17th Meeting, Munich 29–30 November 1989. EPO Doc. SACEPO/XVII/5, pp. 5–6.

31. European Patent Convention, Article 53-b.

32. Council of Europe, Committee of Experts on Patents, 'Memorandum on the Unification of legislation', The Hague, 28 November 1960. (Doc. EXP/Brev (60) 7.)

33. Council of Europe, Committee of Experts on Patents, 'Unification of Laws Convention, Amendment suggested by the Austrian Delegation', Strasbourg, 10 May 1963 (Doc. EXP/Brev. (63) 7).

34. EEC Doc. COM (88)–496, op. cit.

35. EPO, Doc. SACEPO/XVII/5, op. cit., p. 11.

36. W. Lesser, 'Patenting Seeds: What to expect', Dept. of Agricultural Economics, Cornell University, USA, January 1986.

37. EEC Commission, 'A European patent law for Biotechnology', Information Memo, Brussels, October 1988.

38. 'The Battle Raging over Intellectual Property', 1989, op. cit., p. 80.

39. Jack Kloppenburg, 'First The Seed', Cambridge University Press, New York, 1988, pp. 113–116.

40. J. Kloppenburg, 1988, op. cit., p. 298.

41. Example from 'Information Release: Patenting Life to become Legal in the EEC', ICDA Seeds Campaign, Barcelona, 1988.

42. United States Patent Nr. 4,581,847, Hibbert et al., April 15, 1986.

43. UPOV, 'Industrial Patents and Plant Breeders' Rights', Records of a Symposium, UPOV Publication Nr. 342(E), p. 80.

44. C. Fowler et al., 'The Laws of Life ', in *Development Dialogue*, Dag Hammarskjold Foundation, No. 1988: 1–2, Uppsala, 1988, p. 244.

45. *Agbiotechnology News*, January/February 1990.

46. James W. Kent, 'The driving force behind the restructuring of the global seeds industry', in *Seed World*, Vol. 124, No. 7, June 1986.

47. W. Lesser, 1986, op. cit.

48. W. Lesser, 'Anticipation UK Plant Variety Patents', 6, EIPR, 1987, pp. 174–176.

49. Assuming 37% of seed worldwide is home grown and with current total commercial seed market valued at US$ 17 billion.

50. W. Lesser, 1986, op. cit.

51. Agnes Vertier, 'Biotechnologies et Brevets: Report d'Etappe'. CNRS/INRA/MRES, France, February 1989. Unpublished. Survey was done by scanning the database 'EPAT'.

8. Appropriate Biotechnology?

'The high yielding varieties have to be better adapted to my soil, technology and local conditions and not the other way around.'
(Bishnu Thapa, farmer in Nepal)[1]

'That's all very interesting, but my constituency is more on Wall Street than it is in the farmer's field.'
(P. S. Carlson of Crop Genetics Int'l Company)[2]

In the previous chapters we have shown that the bio-revolution will have a profound impact on global agriculture, in developed and in less developed countries. It will affect the position of the Third World, both as exporter of agricultural commodities, and as importer of agro-chemicals and seeds. It will also affect their capability to produce their own food. It is clear that biotechnology, as it is being developed now, is likely to have mainly negative impacts on developing countries. But we have also pointed out that the technology itself could be, at least in principle, a tremendous help in resolving some of the pressing problems that developing nations currently face.

Central to the whole question of the impact of biotechnology is the context in which it is developed. At the moment the technology is progressively falling under private control, mainly to large TNCs. The direction of the research is strongly biased towards a high-tech type of agriculture and the vested interests of industrialized nations. As it stands now, the implementation of the bio-revolution is likely to result in a new international division of labour, a decreased value for raw agricultural materials traditionally produced by the South, and an increased dependence of the Third World on the industrialized nations. Also, if patent protection is widely extended to living matter, the existing advantages of the North in trade relations and technology will be further reinforced.

As a response to the potential of biotechnology, several developing countries have initiated national research and development programmes.

The International Agricultural Research Centres (IARCs) are also developing biotechnology programmes. The work on biotechnology in developing countries should be seen in its proper context. As pointed out in an earlier chapter, it is almost negligible compared to the huge investments in the North. In 1985, only 7.5% of global research and development spendings came from outside the USA/Japan/Europe bloc.[3] With Canada and Australia responsible for most of that already limited share, the Third World emerges as a complete outsider in the bio-revolution. Still, this does not mean that nothing is being done in the South.

The general line of thinking is that Third World countries need to appropriate biotechnology and develop it towards their specific needs. But, then, what is meant by 'appropriation'? It is a concept as broad and misused as often as 'sustainable development'. In this chapter the possibilities and obstacles for using this new and powerful technology for the benefit of the Third World will be examined. First we take a look at the role of the IARCs, the main forces behind that other giant agricultural modernization scheme, the Green Revolution. Then we investigate the efforts that developing countries themselves are currently undertaking to claim at least a small piece of the biotechnological cake.

The IARCs and the privatization of biotechnology

The International Agricultural Research Centers (IARCs), which spearheaded the Green Revolution, have for a long time been seen as the champions of the free exchange of information and technology. Predominantly publicly funded, the IARCs, such as IRRI in the Philippines, CIMMYT in Mexico and CIP in Peru, see their role primarily as providing research results and services to national research programmes in developing countries. Indeed, whatever one thinks of the Green Revolution and the engines behind it, one of the main functions of the IARC system has been to make breeding material available to research institutions in the Third World, which then are supposed further to develop the material and adapt it to local growing conditions.

Most of the IARCs now recognize the immense potential of the new biotechnologies for their work. Many members of the IARC family already use tissue-culture techniques to provide disease-free planting materials and to supplement their germplasm conservation work. CIP in Peru, for example, is storing 5,000 accessions of potato and 2,500 samples of sweet potato in clonal form, using tissue culture. Likewise, CIAT's *in vitro* genebank already holds 3,500 clones of cassava. Tissue-culture work is also being carried out at the International Institute for Tropical Agriculture (IITA) in Nigeria for several African crops. Additionally, so-called 'Wide Cross Programmes', which consist of trying to cross crops with distant relatives using biotechnology, are being carried out at IRRI in the Philippines for rice, at CIMMYT in Mexico for wheat and corn, and at ICRISAT (International Crops Research Institute for the Semi-Arid Tropics) in India for groundnut. Also, ILRAD, the International Laboratory for Research on Animal Diseases in Kenya, is using biotechnology to produce livestock vaccines, while IRRI is doing the same to develop tools for the detection of virus diseases in rice.

But moving into biotechnology is not like setting up a Green Revolution. The IARCs were the inventors and developers of the Green Revolution technology, and operated in the past decades without strong competition from other institutions or the private sector. This is changing rapidly with the emerging new biotechnologies. The privatization and subsequent concentration of biological knowledge in the hands of a few transnational corporations in the North, make the transfer and appropriation of biotechnology for the benefit of developing countries an extremely complex and difficult task. Technically and economically, the Green Revolution was the domain of the IARCs. The new 'high yielding' crop varieties and the techniques to produce them were largely developed at the Centers themselves. For this, the Centers are heavily dependent on the free flow of scientific information and germplasm, and this is precisely what is under direct threat from the highly private character of the new biotechnologies. The Centers are left with the choice of either developing the basic research themselves, or simply striking deals with the companies or institutions in the North. The traditional link with public institutions in North America and Europe is already progressively undermined as those institutions themselves face the effects of privatization of biotech research, and are often already bound to secrecy due to contracts with industry. The building-up of in-house basic biotech research, on the other hand, would mean a substantial shift to more basic research, which could be funded only by transferring funds from more applied research.

A complicating factor is that many public research institutions in industrialized countries are being increasingly excluded from applied research, which is seen as the field where private companies should operate. This is already having profound consequences for the smaller plant-breeders in the US and Europe, who traditionally have depended strongly on the breeders' lines supplied to them by public agricultural research institutions. It will also have implications for the IARCs and biotechnology programmes in developing countries, as they may no longer count on the free availability of high quality expertise from public circles in the North.

Apart from difficulties of access to information and technology, IARCs will also face increasing competition from TNCs for the provision of the end product of the new technology. This factor was largely non-existent during the Green Revolution. With the restructuring of the agro-industry in the North, TNCs are looking for potential high-profit markets in the South.

Many of them already have a solid infrastructure for marketing their pesticides or drugs, and are now using these channels for the distribution of seeds as well. TNCs are especially interested in crops with potentially large markets, such as maize, wheat and rice. TNC involvement in wheat and rice has up to now been relatively limited, because hybrids are not yet commercially available. But extensive research is being conducted to produce commercial hybrids for both wheat and rice. China, for example, is already widely planting hybrid rice and it will not take long before TNCs have perfected the technology. When this breakthrough is made, IARCs and national institutions in developing countries will increasingly find TNCs on their trail when bringing new varieties to the farmer.[4]

These changes in the shape of international agricultural research – restricted access to the new technologies, increased competition on the market, and the characteristics of the new technologies themselves – all mean that IARCs face important policy decisions. Will they focus more on basic biotechnology research or continue with their more applied approach? If, as is likely, the TNCs concentrate on the major crops with global markets, will the IARCs focus more on the 'poor man' crops? Or will they continue to work predominantly on the Green Revolution crops, while perhaps focusing on market niches the TNCs are not interested in? There are many questions, but few answers.

One direction, clearly taking form now, is towards increased IARC-TNC links, similar to the TNC-University contracts in many industrialized countries. Examples of this approach have been given by Richard Sawyer, Director-General of the Peru-based International Potato Centre (CIP). In his opening speech at a conference on the subject he pointed out:

> With the rapid growth of fast-food industry into the developing world, major food processors need local potato varieties that will grow well and provide the accepted standard of processed quality in warm tropical areas . . . Through a collaborative arrangement with some major food processors, we are helping to develop potential varieties that will grow well in the warm tropics and meet rigid quality standards of the fast-food industry.[5]

In other words: the priority is to tailor for the needs of MacDonald's, not for the agronomic and nutritional requirements of farmers.

Sawyer continued with another example of IARC-industry collaboration at his Institute. CIP has identified biological control mechanisms for root-knot nematodes which threaten potato production. Traditionally, the IARCs would disseminate such research results to national research centres in developing countries for further adaptation and improvement. However, according to the Director-General of CIP:

We are not in the business of producing, packaging, and marketing such products. We are in the business of making sure that such products are made available by the private sector . . . Thus, we have a collaborative arrangement with a multinational who is exploring the potential of marketing some of these products . . .[6]

This implies a major shift in policy of IARCs. National research programmes no longer seem to be the main concern, as private industry moves in as a new client for their activities.

Many more examples of such IARC-industry ties are springing up like mushrooms; a selection of these is given in Table 8.1 (see pp. 124–5). Perhaps the most striking example is with CIMMYT in Mexico. This Centre is the crop-oriented IARC with perhaps the closest relationships to the US seed and biotech industry. For a long time it has worked with Pioneer Hi-Bred – the largest seed company in the world – to grow out maize germplasm. Now CIMMYT is embarking on a major collaborative biotech research effort focusing on maize, with major seed companies such as KWS, Limagrain, AMI and Van der Haave. Most of the collaboration with the industry is based on informal agreements, but the open-ended nature of these makes them subject to abuse.[7] Perhaps no one can explain better to what type of future such deals will lead than Donald Duvick, until recently Director of Research with Pioneer Hi-Bred. He stresses that 'any involvement [of the IARCs] with international seed companies will need clear understanding about ownership of resulting commercially valuable products and processes.'[8] No deal is for free!

In the midst of a discussion on how to correct the shortcomings of the Green Revolution, the tendency to sell-out agricultural research for developing countries is hardly encouraging. If the lessons of the Green Revolution are really to be taken seriously, a fundamental reorientation of the research at the IARCs towards the interests of the majority of Third World farmers is imperative. Tying the research to TNCs, as now seems to be happening, points in quite the opposite direction.

Third World national efforts to get involved

The high expectations raised by enthusiastic press reports on the bio-revolution have also reached policy makers in the Third World. National biotechnology research efforts are proliferating rapidly. In Latin America alone, 94 entities, most of them public, are involved in developing the new biotechnologies, according to a recent survey.[9] About half of them are located in Brazil and Argentina (see Graph 8.1) although this does not necessarily reflect total commitment by a country, as the size of biotechnology projects varies considerably.

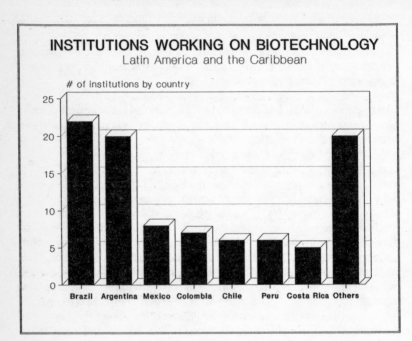

Of all Latin American nations, Brazil is generally seen as the country which puts most money into developing biotechnology. The country's 'National Biotechnology Programme' (PRONAB), initiated in 1981, has agriculture, animal husbandry, energy and health as priority fields. In agriculture, objectives include nitrogen fixation, crop resistance to adverse ecological conditions, increased photosynthetic efficiency of forage crops and improvement of biological pest control.[10] In the field of agricultural biotechnology, perhaps more important is the Brazilian Public Corporation for Agricultural Research (EMBRAPA) of the Ministry of Agriculture and its National Research Centre of Genetic Resources (CENARGEN), which have a substantial part of their research and development dedicated to biotechnology.

One major concern, not only in the case of Brazil, is that a substantial part of Third World biotechnology research is directed towards the major cash crops, which are normally controlled by large estate owners. An example is the biotech research for Brazil's 'miracle' alcohol programme in the energy field. Using sugar-cane as the main raw material to produce alcohol for fuel, the country now derives 28% of its energy from biomass. Tissue-culture is used to produce sugar-cane with high yields and tolerance to herbicides, and the fermentation processes to turn the sugar into alcohol

Table 8.1
The privatization of the IARCs and related institutions

Inst.	Activity	Private company involvement	Patent policy
CIP (Peru)	Develop potato varieties for fast food industries	'Collaborative agreements with some major food processors'	CIP's general policy is to go for patenting
	Biological control of root knot nematodes with fungi	Contract with Abbot Laboratories for marketing	
CIMMYT (Mexico)	Grow out of maize collection	Pioneer Hi-Bred, the lagest seed company in the world, was permitted to grow out and keep a copy of CIMMYT's maize germplasm	'Collaborative projects between CIMMYT and the private sector are not only desirable, but essential.'
	'CIMMYT Maize Network', to foster application of molecular genetics to maize plant breeding	Network consists of several institutions, including European seed companies such as KWS (FRG), Limagrain (FR), AMI (Italy) and Van Der Haave (NL). In the USA, contacts being developed with Pioneer and Agrigenetics	It seems that there is no clear patent policy CIMMYT, despite its strong involvement with the private sector
	'Latin American Maize Project' consisting of 12 countries (including USA), to evaluate genetic maize diversity. CIMMYT's role in this project is not clear	Wilfred Salhuana, of Pioneer Hi-Bred, is senior adviser to the project, and has thus first sight of all evaluated material	

IRRI (Phil.)	New method to extract insecticide from Neem tree leaves	No direct corporate involvement, but there is a discussion on whether to patent	IRRI policy seems to be not to patent, although debate is increasing as IRRI's work becomes more and more interesting for corporations
	IRRI hybrid rice is being field tested. To be distributed to farmers in the early 1990s	No direct company involvement, but interference is expected in the future as TNCs are working in the same area: Occidental Petroleum (USA), Mitsui Toatsu and Mitsubishi (Japan)	
ICIPE (Kenya)	Screening of African plants for insecticide activity	Contract with ENEA (Italian chemical company) whereby ICIPE sends all natural chemicals screening results to ENEA for further testing. Any resulting profit will be divided by ICIPE and ENEA	ICIPE already patented outcome of its research. Tendency is to increase patent activity as a means for extra income from royalties
ILRAD (Kenya)	Vaccine production, especially for 'East Coast Fever' in cattle	Agreement being negotiated with 'major American company' (probably Monsanto), where company brings in expertise in antigen production. Still unclear who will take care of production and distribution of outcome	ILRAD has an active policy to patent the outcome of its research

Sources: USAID, *Strengthening Collaboration in Biotechnology*, Conference Proceedings, USAID, Washington, April 1989 (several contributions); F. Buttel, M. Kenney, *Institutional Constraints to Biotechnological Innovation in International Agricultural Research and Development*, report prepared for the Rockefeller Foundation (draft), New York, September 1987; several annual reports of the IARCs.

are being improved by using enzyme technology.[11] The darker side of the story is that the alcohol programme, while having saved the country an estimated $1 billion in energy expenses over the past decade, has had a tremendous negative impact on the rural poor. Brazil's land area devoted to sugar-cane has risen from 1.5 million hectares in 1972 to 3.8 million in 1985. Much of this expansion has occurred at the cost of fertile land traditionally dedicated to food production by small farmers.[12]

Nitrogen fixation is another priority area in Brazil's biotechnology efforts. EMBRAPA is selecting improved *Rhizobia* strains to increase the nitrogen fixation capacity of legumes. While *Rhizobia* strains could be applied to a whole range of legumes, a full 99% of all inoculants are used with soybean alone, another cash crop grown mainly for export. This fertilizer-saving technology would be perfectly feasible on the country's main staple food: *Feijao* or black bean.[13]

Brazil is also celebrating considerable success in the production of bio-pesticides. But, again, the vast majority of the work is directed towards the main cash crops. EMBRAPA commercially produces a viral insecticide to control a major insect pest in the soybean plantations (locally known as *largarta de soya*). Another virus is being investigated to control an insect pest in sugar-cane plantations.[14] A third major project is the use of a fungus to control spittle-bug infections in sugar-cane, soybean, coffee and pastures.[15]

The heavy focus of agricultural research on cash crops has contributed to an extremely biased growth in production. While between 1967 and 1977 there was a 13% increase in the productivity of export crops, food crops increased by only 1.7%. This approach exacerbates Brazil's iniquitous pattern of land ownership – 10% of landowners control 80% of the land, and about one million small farmers are thrown off their plots each year.[16] Because research is not directed to the needs of the vast majority of small farmers, biotechnology is likely to reinforce this skewed pattern of resources allocation in favour of large landholders and export crops, to the detriment of food production and the rural poor.

Another country carrying out extensive biotechnology research is Mexico. Several universities include biotechnology in their research programmes, especially focusing on tissue-culture. According to a survey by the Mexican University UAM, much of the agriculture-related biotechnology research is focused on tissue-culture of fruits and flowers for export.[17] Tissue-culture is also used to mass propagate élite varieties of the agave cactus by the Tequila Cuervo company to ensure a continuous supply of the raw material for this popular drink. But the flagship of Mexico's biotechnology efforts is at the National Biotechnology Centre, where highly sophisticated genetic engineering work, using recombinant DNA technology, is being carried out. Under the leadership of Dr Francisco Bolivar, former employee of the US biotech firm Genentech, the centre focuses on four projects: human insulin; human interferon; DNA polymorphism for racial history; and the production of xanthan gum in micro-organisms.

A report prepared for the Rockefeller Foundation questions the relevance of such projects for the majority of the Mexicans.[18] Animal-derived insulin is available and can be produced in Mexico. Interferon is also a questionable target, as the outcome of this work is likely to be too expensive for the majority of a population that cannot afford even basic health care. Research on DNA polymorphism amongst Mexican Indians might be interesting, but what are the practical applications?

> What benefits will this program yield to the vast majority of the Mexicans? . . . Problems such as infant diarrhea or other diseases of the poor would seem much better targets for Mexican biotechnology research.[19]

The work on xanthan gum, which is used as a lubricant for oil-drilling, was initially funded by PEMEX, a Mexican petrochemical industry. When the project was ready for scaling up, however, PEMEX dropped it. The greatest interest in the project then came from Japanese and US multinationals: 'hardly the segment of the world economy that needs LDC-subsidized technical assistance.'[20]

Perhaps to a larger extent than in Latin America, several Asian developing countries are making efforts to use biotechnology in agricultural development. Table 8.2 lists the most important ones, together with the main institutions involved and their general objectives. China and India are reportedly amongst the lead countries in agricultural biotechnology, while the Republic of Korea is stronger in industrial biotechnology with important participation from the private sector. China has been especially successful with the development of high-yielding hybrid rice, which is now sown to over one-third of its total rice acreage of 30 million hectares.[21] China also plants 10% of its potato acreage to virus-free, tissue-cultured potatoes resulting in substantial yield increases. Tissue-culture is also used to mass propagate sugar-cane, grapes, Chinese fir, red banana, orange and pineapple.[22] China's hybrid rice technology has been the subject of controversy as it licensed exclusive rights for the technology to two US TNCs (Cargill and Occidental Petroleum). The technology has subsequently been patented in the USA and the companies are unwilling to release the know-how as commercialization has not yet proved to be feasible.[23] Dr R. Singh, from FAO's office in Bangkok, strongly criticizes this licensing practice of China. He thinks it has 'locked [up] one of the most relevant technologies and set of materials highly demanded by other developing countries.'[24]

Thailand is credited, by a draft report drawn up for the World Bank, with having well-formulated policies on biotechnology with a reasonable level of funding.[25] The National Centre for Genetic Engineering and Biotechnology was set up by the government in 1983 as the main policy, support and co-ordination centre. There are four affiliated laboratories and the

Table 8.2
Biotechnology programmes in Asia (selected countries)

Country	Institution	Work
China	National Center for Biotechnology, several other institutions	Increased cereal output; improved food production; biotech output 1.5% of GNP to be increased fourfold by the year 2000.
India	Department of Biotechnology (of Ministry of Science and Tech.) (1986). Also private companies	Nitrogen-fixation; bio-pesticides; pest-resistant crops; better nutrition; tissue culture
Indonesia	National Centre for Biotechnology (1986)	Food self-sufficiency; enhanced export; employment
Malaysia	Biotechnology Expert Group (of NCRD)	Tissue culture & rDNA; biomass conversion; improvement of traditional food processing
Philippines	National Institute of Biotechnology (BIOTECH)	Crop improvement; import substitution; farming systems; resource conservation
Korea	National Genetic Engineering Centre (1985)	Self-sufficiency in food; increased competitiveness in biological products; eliminate pests and diseases
Thailand	National Centre for Genetic Engineering and Biotechnology (1983)	Reduce cost of production; diversify crops and products; increase production of value-added products

Source: Dr R. B. Sing, *Current Status and Future Prospects of Plant Biotechnology in Developing Countries of Asia*, paper presented at CTA/FAO Symposium on 'Plant Biotechnologies for Developing Countries', Luxembourg, 26–30 June 1989.

centre also supports over 30 different projects at universities and other research centres in Thailand.[26] Examination of the agricultural projects funded by the Centre (Table 8.3) shows a strong bias towards cash crops and/or large-scale farming. The work on animals focuses on embryo transfer in dairy cattle to increase milk production, and hormone technology on buffaloes to increase fertility. The latter 'will provide a basis for more successful artificial insemination and embryo transfer.'[27] This high-tech research is unlikely to benefit small farmers, as they use local animal races. In crop agriculture, tissue-culture work focuses on oil-palm, rubber, rattan and cut flowers – all cash crops predominantly destined for export. The results of the work on disease-free potato planting materials is 'potentially suitable for large commercial scale production' according to those responsible for the research.[28] Perhaps the only research with promising potential for small farmers and food crops is the work on compost and on bio-fertilizers, but that will depend on how the government makes these new technologies available. Such priority choices seem to reflect the government's concern with commodity exports rather than with food production and the position of the small farmers in the country.

The Philippines made a considerable effort to get involved in biotechnology when it set up the National Institute of Biotechnology and Applied Microbiology (BIOTEC) within the agricultural university UPLB (Los Banos) in 1979 with splendid facilities. Since then, the Institute has suffered from unreliable and diminishing financial support from the government.[29] BIOTEC has a large number of projects, but few senior staff to lead them. Of the nearly 200 staff working in or affiliated to the Institute in 1984, there were only five or six PhDs employed full time.[30] Nevertheless, it maintained a programme oriented toward the rural sector. Its focus is on four interdisciplinary research programmes: bio-fuels; nitrogen fixation; food fermentation processes; and tissue-culture. These seem to be areas with concrete applications for small farmers, but Saturnini Halos, from the University of the Philippines, found that their usefulness for small farmers was limited by several factors.[31] The production of fuel from biomass, for example, has been largely directed to large farmers, as initial capital requirements are too high for peasants. Also, a bio-pesticide killing small worm pests in several crops was developed by the University, but the production and distribution has been handed over to one company. This resulted in a monopoly situation where the price is still too high to be accessible to small farmers. In general, the study concludes, 'No conscious effort is locally made in directing technology development to different types of farmers.'[32] This normally means that the technology ends up in the hands of only one type of farmer: the one who can pay for it.

A major problem with the development of Third World biotechnology programmes is the lack of financial resources and scientific infrastructure. One institution trying to do something about this is the International Centre for Genetic Engineering and Biotechnology (ICGEB). Launched at the beginning of the 1980s by the UN Industrial Development Organization (UNIDO), this Centre aims to be a 'centre of excellence' for biotechnology research directed at developing countries. ICGEB's concept is unique and challenging, but its formation has been thwarted by intense political controversy and debate. Initial resistance came especially from the USA and Japan who feared that the Centre might challenge their worldwide dominating position in biotech research. The political squabbling resulted in a situation in which the Centre's location was split between Italy and India, and the whole operation is still suffering from serious under-funding. Another problem is that the main proponents in the Third World agricultural biotechnology scheme, CGIAR and FAO, have been largely absent from the gestation of the Centre. Many observers now question the

Table 8.3
Biotechnology in Thailand (projects related to agriculture)

Institution	Project	Comment
Chula-longkorn Univ.	Cultivation of Shitake Mushrooms	Production of compost, for export and domestic consumption
Chula-longkorn Univ.	Nitrogen fixation in rice	Focus on N-fixing bacteria
Chula-longkorn Univ.	Steroid immunization of swamp buffaloes	Objective is to increase fertility of the buffaloes
ISTR	Algae for N-fixation in rice	Also studies on effect of salt and pesticides
ISTR	Fungi to increase phosphate uptake	Research on relation of fungi and N-fixing bacteria
Kasetsart Univ.	Disease-free potato seed	'Suitable for large commercial scale production'
Kasetsart Univ.	Embryo transfer in dairy cattle	To raise milk production and improve cattle breeding
Kasetsart Univ.	*In vitro* conservation	Special focus on plant important for Thai culture
Kasetsart Univ.	Micro-organisms for compost production	Microbes are screened for effectiveness in compost product
Kasetsart Univ.	Tissue culture for cut flowers	Mass production of temperate cut flowers for export
Kasetsart Univ.	Tissue culture of Rattan palm	Rattan is used for furniture, and exported esp. to Japan
Mahidol Univ.	Strain selection of terrestrial snails	Thai snails are important for export
Mahidol Univ.	Tissue culture of medicinal plants	Screening for high diosgenin production
National Centre	Plant Tissue Culture Network	Organization of workshops and data bases
Songkla Univ.	High-yielding rubber clones	Evaluation of rubber tree at seedling stage
Songkla Univ.	Tissue culture of oil-palm	For mass propagation and quality improvement

Source: Y. Yuthavong et al., 'National Programs in Biotechnology for Thailand and other Southeast Asian countries', in *Strengthening Collaboration in Biotechnology* Conference Proceedings, 17–21 April 1988, USAID, Washington, 1989.

viability of this operation to contribute substantially to the biotechnology research efforts of developing countries.[33]

Perhaps the most serious problem with ICGEB is that it seems to fall in the same trap as many national biotechnology programmes. There is a high degree of uncertainty about its specific goals. With its broad and all-encompassing mandate it runs the risk of doing a little bit of everything without really making a substantial contribution to anything. More seriously, some of its research priorities are extremely questionable with respect to their usefulness for Third World countries. Of the five agricultural research priorities of ICGEB at New Delhi, one relates to the production of herbicide tolerant crops.[34] Apart from the fact that herbicide tolerance is already extensively researched by TNCs in the North, it is doubtful that this will have much relevance for the majority of Third World farmers who cannot afford to use herbicides, not to mention its potentially harmful impact on health and the environment. Another research priority relates to the long-term goal to transfer genes of *Amaranthus* coding for high protein content to crops such as rice and wheat.[35] *Amaranthus* is an important crop for many subsistence farmers in the Third World. While work on increased protein content of rice and wheat is important, one might ask why ICGEB does not also focus on improving the *Amaranthus* crop itself and thus promote its use in farming systems. Such research might prove to be more beneficial in the short run to the many small farmers who grow the crop already.

The central point for the success of Third World biotechnology programmes is that research priorities must be very carefully defined in tune with the specific needs of the majority of the population. It does not help for developing countries simply to join the high-tech biotechnology race that is taking place now among the industrialized countries. Focusing instead on low-tech, low-cost techniques with clear application possibilities for the majority of the farmers might seem an obvious choice, but the opposite is often happening. One researcher, after visiting several biotechnology centres in Latin America, put it this way:

> Technically simple projects such as these are not well supported. It is scientists with extensive credentials, following the US model, who impress politicians and continue to extract considerable funding, while accomplishing little that is applicable to the needs of the vast majority of the citizens.[36]

This is in fact one of the crucial points in counteracting biotechnology as it is now being developed in the interest of the industrialized nations. The commitment to support biotechnology programmes in the Third World must not be a tool merely to enhance national prestige without consequential fall-out, but should translate genuine will to attenuate poverty and hunger. For this, precise objectives that are coherent with overall agricultural development policies must be defined. This means that the programmes can succeed only if there is a clear understanding of the problems faced by the rural and urban poor, as well as a realistic assessment of the possibilities offered by biotechnology to help solve them. In many cases this also means that the programmes should be accompanied by socio-economic reforms to strengthen the position of the poor. In any case, priorities should be set in consultation with grass-roots organizations and other NGOs, who often have a clear understanding of the situation and a considerable knowledge of the local resources. Only then can one start talking about 'appropriate biotechnology'.

Notes and references

1. Quoted in Purna Chhetri, 'Bishnu's and Kheti's sustainable farm in Nepal', in *ILEIA Newsletter*, Vol. 4, No. 1, Leusden, March 1988, p. 17.

2. P. S. Carlson, 'One Company's Attempt to Commercialize an Agricultural Biotechnology Technology', in *Strengthening Collaboration in Biotechnology*, Conference Proceedings, USAID, Washington, April 1989, p. 414.

3. G. Persley, *Agricultural Biotechnology: Opportunities for International Development*. Draft Synthesis Report, World Bank (with ISNAR, AIDAB and ACIAR), May 1989, p. 68.

4. See Henk Hobbelink, 'Agricultural Biotechnology and the Third World'. Paper presented to the Conference 'Development Related Research: The Role of the Netherlands'. University of Gröningen, 29–31 March, 1989.

5. Richard Sawyer, 'The CGIAR Centres, Building Bridges of Collaboration through Biotechnology', in *Strengthening Collaboration in Biotechnology*, 1989, op. cit., p. 17.

6. Ibid., p. 18.

7. F. Buttel, M. Kenney, 'Institutional Constraints to Biotechnological Innovation in International Agricultural Research and Development'. Report prepared for the Rockefeller Foundation. (Draft), New York, September 1987.

8. Donald Duvick, 'Research Collaboration and Technology Transfer', in *Strengthening Collaboration in Biotechnology*, 1989, op. cit., p. 27.

9. H. Chaverra, 'The Current Status of Plant Biotechnologies in LDCs: Latin America and the Caribbean'. Paper presented to the CTA/FAO Symposium 'Plant Biotechnologies for LDCs', Luxembourg, 26–30 June 1989.

10. 'The Brazilian National Biotechnology Programme', in *Bio/Technology*, May 1984, p. 421.

11. Ibid., p. 426.

12. J. de Souza Silva, 'Biotechnology in Brazil and Prospects for South-South Cooperation', in *Biotechnology Revolution and the Third World*, RIS, New Delhi, 1988, pp. 420–42.

13. Pablo Bifani, *New Biotechnologies for Rural Development*, ILO Working Papers No. 195, ILO, Geneva, 1989, p. 29.

14. *Diatrea saccharalis*.

15. P. Bifani, 1989, op. cit., pp. 46–8.

16. J. de Souza Silva, op. cit., 1988.

17. G. Arroyo, S. Arias, 'Lineamientos Estrategicos para un Desarrollo Endigeno: La contribucion de la biotecnologia', in *ECA*, July 1987.

18. F. Butel, M. Kenney, 1987, op. cit., p. 93.

19. Ibid.

20. Ibid.

21. H. Pearce, 'Chinese Super-rice in the Balance', in *Panoscope*, No. 16, January 1990, p. 4.

22. R. Singh, 'Current Status and Future Prospects of Plant Biotechnology in LDCs of Asia'. Paper presented to a CTA/FAO Symposium 'Plant Biotechnolgoies for LDCs', Luxembourg, 26–30 June 1989, p. 20.

23. H. Pearce, 1990, op. cit.

24. R. Singh, 1989, op. cit., p. 57.

25. G. Persley, op. cit., p. 84.

26. Y. Yuthavong et al., 'National Programs in Biotechnology for Thailand and other S.E. Asian Countries', in *Strengthening Collaboration in Biotechnology*, 1989, op. cit., p. 40.

27. Ibid., p. 45.

28. Ibid.

29. S. C. Halos, *Biotechnology Trends: A Threat to Philippine Agriculture?*, ILO Working Papers No. 193, ILO, January 1989.

30. F. Buttel, M. Kenney, 1987, op. cit., p. 99.

31. S. Halos, 1989, op. cit., pp. 10–16.

32. Ibid., p.15

33. F. Butel, M. Kenney, 1987, op. cit., pp. 77–83.

34. K. Venkataraman, 'The role of UNIDO', in *Biotechnology Revolution and the Third World*, 1988, op. cit., p. 375.

35. Ibid., pp. 375–6.

36. Martin Kenney, 'Reflections on a Visit to Latin American Biotechnology Research Institutes' in *GeneWatch*, Vol. 2, No. 3, September/October, 1985.

9. The Original Biotechnologist

'In Africa there are lots of unsophisticated farmers. You can't even expect them to drive a tractor straight.'
(Norman Goldfarb, Chairman of Calgene, USA)[1]

While visiting a friend a few years ago, I found myself roaming around on the island of Zanzibar, just off the coast of Tanzania. One farmer insisted on showing me around. After quite a walk through what seemed to me to be a forest, he stopped and asked my opinion. I wasn't quite sure about what, until I realized that I was standing in the middle of one of his fields or *shambas* as he calls them. What my Northern mind had conceived as just a bit more of the same bush that covers the island, was actually a carefully designed and cultivated farmer's field. Palm trees, bananas and fruit trees were growing tall above numerous annual crops, most of which I did not even know the name of. Patiently, he explained in extreme detail why which plant was growing where and what use it had. Since then I am a bit more careful when looking at bushes along the roadside in Third World countries.

Much of this book has focused on what is known as the *new* biotechnologies and their implications for agriculture. Genetic engineering, cell fusion, tissue-culture, enzyme technologies and the like, will bring tremendous changes to the agriculture we now know. Very often during discussion on this issue, the question is raised as to what type of biotechnology would be beneficial for small farmers in developing countries. Before even trying to start formulating an answer, it is important to recognize the profound complexity and high level of adaptation to local circumstances of many indigenous farming practices. It is crucial to evaluate such farming systems on their own merits: to what extent they meet the need of local communities, now and in the future, and to what degree they provide a sustainable basis for national agricultural development. Only if analysed in that context does a possible answer to the question whether and how the new biotechnologies can contribute to sustainable farming make sense.

Most local farming practices are based on an enormous degree of diversity, be it cultural, biological or economic. This diversity is often regarded by 'modern' scientists as a consequence of inefficient traditional farming, rather than the prerequisite for survival and development. Some experts would agree that such systems might work at the community level, but argue that they cannot produce the food for an ever-increasing urban population as well. The International Centre for Tropical Agriculture in Colombia, for example, has tried to redirect some of its work to the needs of small farmers; but some researchers at the Centre remain sceptical. CIAT rice breeder Peter Jennings says that the focus at CIAT 'is much more on the consumer than on the farmer, and I'm not convinced we should focus on the marginal producer'.[2] What Jennings does not seem to realize, is that in many developing countries these 'marginal producers' form the vast majority of the population. It is this line of thinking that reinforces the tendency of small farmers to move off (or simply be thrown off) their land and turn up in the poverty stricken slums of large cities, only to increase the number of urban consumers who need food from elsewhere.

Rarely is it recognized that local farming systems provide the very basis of a sustainable form of agriculture, optimizing the long-term use of the locally available natural resources, minimizing the need for external chemical inputs, while at the same time providing for a reasonably stable output of food, medicines and shelter. The generations of farmers who have developed, maintained and improved these practices are the 'original biotechnologists'. The new biotechnologists, and agents for agricultural development policies in general, should take these systems as a point of departure for possible further improvement. The interdependency and complexity of the various elements of people's biotechnology is so deep that modern science has often overlooked it. Worse is that by introducing 'improvements' based on a reality cut up into manageable pieces, the very basis of farming systems that have proved their value for centuries is being undermined and sometimes completely destroyed. The new biotechnologists, however learned they might be in their specialism at the molecular and genetic level, can have something positive to offer to the rural and urban poor only if their solutions enhance the sustainable basis of farming practices. But grasping the complexity and importance of diversity, rather than merely regarding it as raw material for research, is very difficult. It has never been the strongest point of scientists, who tend to work more with microscopes than with local farmers.

One particular point that is difficult to understand for many of us who rely on local diets of cornflakes, wheat bread and potatoes, is the immense variety of plants that are used for food in many parts of the world. Villagers living at the foot of Mount Elgon in Western Kenya use at least 100 different species of vegetables and fruits in their diet. Some of them are actively cultivated, others collected from the wild.[3] Mexico's Huastec Indians cultivate, in a mixture of home gardens, agricultural fields and forest plots, some 300 different plant species. In a typical village garden in West Java it is not difficult to find 100 or more different plant species, all used for specific needs: food, medicine, building materials, fuel-wood, and so on.[4] Also, the vast local knowledge of plants and their uses is truly astonishing. The Tzeltals in Mexico recognize over 1,200 different plant species, while Hanunoo farmers in the Philippines know more than 1,600. When scientists came out of a forest in Botswana with a collection of 211 different rare plants, they were amazed to discover that village women knew all but five.[5]

Diversity for production

Indigenous farmers in developing countries translate this deep understanding of different plants and animals and their uses to farming systems which are very much adapted to their own circumstances. In Sierra Leone, in a village called Mogbuama, farmers produce their main staple food, rice, on a range of different plots. Some of them are higher up on the hills, consisting of free draining gravelly soils. Others, on the lower slopes, have more sandy soils, while yet others consist of seasonally water-logged swamp soils in the bottom of the valley. Mogbuama farmers have developed a whole series of different rice varieties for their soils and use them in such a way that the combination fits their needs best. Every family is keen to have some early ripening rice in order to have food before the main harvest starts. This is planted where the swamp and the valley meet, and harvested before the river overspills its bank. The rice varieties that take longer but generally yield better are planted higher up the slopes, while flood tolerant varieties planted down in the wetlands take longest to ripen but require minimal labour input. A researcher who did fieldwork in the village counted 49 different rice varieties in use, each of them with specific qualities. Risk-spreading and labour diversification are some of the main factors behind the choice of the varieties, which is also the reason why Mogbuama farmers are not using any of the modern varieties that are being pushed by the development agencies.[6]

Farmers know about local soils, pests, diseases, weather patterns and other agronomic conditions they have to cope with. They are also the ones who realize best in which time labour requirements are high and how to adapt their agricultural practices in such a way that all the work can be realistically completed. Most of all, they know how to spread risks. Sometimes Northern farmers wonder why many farms in developing countries have so many widely scattered, postage-stamp size fields. As with the Mogbuama farms, in many cases there is a logical reason for it. Scattered fields reduce the risk of total crop failure. Especially in mountainous areas, they allow for diversification: different crops have different problems and potentials at different altitudes. They also result in an extension of the harvest time: a few metres of elevation can make a few days' difference in maturation of the crop. It is this, which one observer called 'the art of vertical thinking', that is lacking in many modernization schemes.[7]

Farmers are good at horizontal thinking too. In the same plot, indigenous farmers often plant many different varieties of the same crop, each of them with specific characteristics. In the Andes, for example, farmers cultivate as many as 50 different potato varieties.[8] Anibal Correo, a potato farmer in Ecuador, explains:

> In a dry year maybe some of the varieties don't yield so much, but then we still have the other potatoes which can put up with some dryness. In a wet year, it can be just the opposite, and we're glad of the potatoes that aren't so liable to rot.[9]

There are other varieties resistant to frost and yet again others that resist cutworms. Also, nutritional and storage qualities come in as important selection criteria. Correo briefly tried new potato varieties offered by agronomists coming to his village, but dropped them when cutworms started eating away at the harvest. On the other side of the globe, in Nepal, Bishnu Tapa and his wife tend to agree. They tried a modern potato variety and were quite impressed with its initial growth; but it did not last long. Potato blight devastated their enthusiasm for the high-yielding variety; the mosaic of varieties they had been using for a long time largely resisted the disease.[10]

Multiple cropping, multiple benefits

The high level of sophistication of indigenous farming systems becomes really apparent when farmers start planting different crops together on the same plot. In what looks to many agronomists like a total mess, many farmers get the maximum out of their tiny fields by combining different crops that complement each other efficiently. To a large extent ignored by 'modern science', farmers, for centuries, have been practising what became known as mixed cropping, intercropping, or multiple cropping. Systems can be as simple as a typical maize-bean association and as complex as a tropical forest where up to 20 crops are grown in the same plot. In Africa, for example, 98% of all cowpeas – the continent's most important legume – are grown in combination with other crops. In Nigeria alone, over 80% of all cropland is given over to mixed cropping. Farmers in India use more than 80 crops in multiple cropping combinations.[11] When Nairobi-based ICIPE, an international centre that studies insect pests, did a survey amongst farmers in Western Kenya, it found over 200 crop combinations in that region alone.[12] The advantages are tremendous, especially for small farmers. ICIPE drew its conclusions: 'If people are doing this despite official instructions to the opposite, there must be something very important to it.'[13]

One important element in such systems can be the use of green manure. Without using any chemical fertilizer, farmers on the north coast of Honduras obtain double the average national yield by sowing velvet bean in their maize crop. The bean is sown a month or two after planting the maize. When the maize is harvested, the beans take over and form a massive green canopy of up to 20 centimetres thick that covers the soil. The next maize crop is planted directly through the mulch which is formed from the bean crop layer. Apart from obtaining the benefits of the nitrogen fixed by the bean, soil erosion is prevented and the soil structure is improved. Also the bean mulch suppresses weed growth, thus eliminating the need for herbicides or manual weeding.[14]

Intercropping can also provide for a highly effective means of pest control at virtually no cost. A study on plant-feeding insects showed that 60% of all species tested were less abundant in mixtures than in monocultures.[15] In Colombia, it was found that beans grown with maize had 25% fewer leaf-hoppers and 45% fewer leaf-beetles than monocultured beans; the maize had 23% fewer army worms as well.[16] Problems with fungal and virus diseases also diminished considerably. Cassava interplanted with bean reduced fungal infections on both crops, while virus infections of cowpea diminish when this crop is grown with cassava or plantain.[17] Before pesticides even existed, farmers took notice and developed their strategies. But then, intercropping is only one of the elements in farmers' strategies to minimize crop losses due to pests and diseases. Use of local resistant crop varieties, proper seed and land preparation, rotation techniques and plant extracts, are just some of the others. Farmers attending training courses on crop protection in Cameroon, for example, told their instructors that they were having excellent results in combating several insect pests by using extracts of Jimson Weed, castor oil, 'God's tobacco' and papaya, to mention just a few.[18]

But perhaps the most challenging feature of many of the mixed cropping systems is that they optimize the use of natural resources without destroying them. Interplanted crops tend to cover the soil better, thus avoiding erosion, while at the same time repressing undesirable weeds. Different crops need different nutrients and have different ways of finding them. Some send their roots deep down, while others stay in the top layer of the soil. Together they form excellent partners while obtaining up to twice the level of nutrients from the soil compared to their monocultured counterparts. At the same time, multiple cropping systems often bring far more fertility and structure back to the soil via plant residues. This is especially the case when legumes are part of the system as they increase the nitrogen fixing capacity of the crop system. The closer a farming system comes to a natural ecosystem, the more likely it is to be sustainable. While scientists still try to grasp the meaning and function of typical two-crop interplantings, farmers in, for example, Nigeria, have developed systems of tree and crop production that reflect the natural multi-storeyed structure of a rain forest. *SPORE*, the newsletter from the Technical Centre for Agriculture and Rural Dissemination (CTA), explains what they consist of:

> Breadfruit, Raffia and pear trees are planted below taller coconut and oil palms. A mixture of shorter trees such as mango, lime and kolanut come next, followed by a lower layer of bananas, plantains and papaya. Cassava, cocoyam and pepper bushes grow to about two metres. Maize, groundnuts and other vegetables are grown in small clearings . . . This farming system is virtually self-sustaining. A relatively large population is being supported on fairly poor soil, by combining livestock, use of organic fertilizers, high crop diversity and control of soil erosion.[19]

Perhaps the most important misconception about these complex farming systems is the claim that they tend to produce less than monocultures. They might produce quantitatively less of one and the same crop, but generally the combinations yield far more. Researchers in Mexico established that

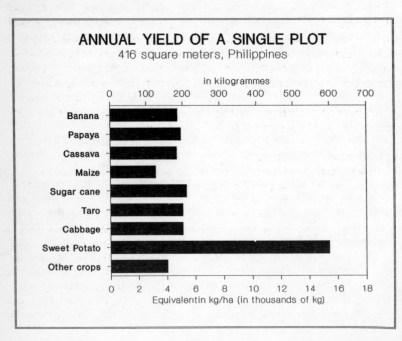

ANNUAL YIELD OF A SINGLE PLOT
416 square meters, Philippines

Table 9.1
Ten reasons for multiple cropping

1. Substantial increase of total crop yields compared to monoculture

2. Increased stability and less occurrence of crop disasters. Spreading of risk, guaranteeing constant food supply.

3. Spread of harvest over longer time period, thus optimizing labour requirements and providing for food supply over an extended period.

4. Reduction of pests and diseases due to diverse ecosystems in the field.

5. Reduction of weed invasion due to early and optimum soil coverage.

6. Reduction of soil erosion through better cover from sun and rain.

7. Improved soil fertility and structure as more crop residues return to the soil and Nitrogen fixing plants are used.

8. Optimized use of environmental resources (water, soil nutrients, solar radiation).

9. Space is provided for crops needed in small quantities (spices, medicinal plants, etc.).

10. Less to no requirement for external chemical inputs.

1.73 hectares of land would be needed to obtain the same amount of food as one hectare of a mixture of maize, bean and squash.[20] Bolivian farmers intercrop beans, potatoes and lupins and in virtually all cases obtain higher yields compared to monocropping. Additionally, viral and fungal diseases are significantly lower in the mixed cultures and the intercropped potatoes store better.[21] Graph 9.1 shows the extent of one year's production on a small poly-cultured plot of about 400 square metres in the Philippines in which 12 different crops produce over two tonnes of fruits, vegetables, spices and cash crops – a yield of about 50,000 kilograms per hectare! No hybrid seeds, irrigation or mechanical farm implements, and only a small amount of chicken manure, were used.[22]

Often ignored in official production statistics are the multiple uses that crops can have. While a typical local vegetable can be grown mainly for its leaves, its roots might have medicinal properties. Shrubs and trees, apart from producing food, can provide foodstuff for animals and timber for building and fuel. Perhaps the prime example of a multiple use crop is the coconut, 'the tree of a hundred uses'. While production statistics mainly focus on the industrial products such as oil, local farmers use the crop for a whole range of purposes. Coconut flesh and milk are consumed fresh, the copra is used to produce oil for local use, the trunk is used as construction material, the palm as thatch or to make brooms and baskets, the shell as fuel and the sap of the tree is the basis for local wine production.

Diversity is the key element in all these different farming practices. There is a tremendous degree of biological diversity in the number of crops and the amount of different varieties of the same species used. There is also a broad diversity in the different strategies applied to maintain and improve soil structure and fertility, to minimize crop losses, or to combine plant and animal production. Up to now we have especially focused on crop production, but often the very core of many indigenous farming systems is the combination of animal and crop production. In most industrialized countries the tendency has been neatly to separate these. But combined plant and animal production provides numerous benefits, as animal dung is brought back to the field while additional output is obtained. Many rice farmers raise fish in their paddies, harvesting up to 500 kilograms per hectare of additional protein-rich food at virtually no cost. Apart from providing meat and milk, buffaloes provide traction power, natural fertilizer and a whole series of other benefits.[23] Invisible in most production statistics, this mixed food production at all levels forms the backbone of most indigenous farming practices.

Biotechnology for the people

If one looks at some of the literature on how indigenous Third World farmers have developed their agriculture, or if one simply walks around in one of their tiny and untidy-looking plots, the general feeling is of awe and amazement. The complexity, interdependence, and high level of sophistication of many farming systems deserves respect indeed. When scanning through journals and scientific papers reporting the latest breakthroughs in the new biotechnologies, the feeling is similar. Still, something does not match up in those two experiences. The original and the new biotechnologists seem to use a different type of genius. The first one is based on a broad and holistic approach to a specific agronomic and socio-economic situation. The latter tends to look for universal solutions deep down at the molecular level, sometimes coming up with breathtaking examples of engineering capabilities. One wonders whether those two approaches are compatible and to what extent one could supplement and strengthen the other.

That the technology from the original biotechnologist helps the new biotechnologist is beyond doubt. Many of the two million or so seed samples now stored in gene banks worldwide originate from the fields of Third World farmers. As pointed out earlier, this forms the precious raw material for the new biotechnologist. As well, scientific missions in search of landraces or wild material also collect the knowledge of indigenous people about them. Perfect South-North technology transfer, and for free!

The question to what extent the new biotechnologies can strengthen indigenous farming systems is far more complex. First there is the problem, stressed throughout this book, that this new set of powerful technologies is predominantly developed in and for industrialized countries and is rapidly becoming the exclusive property of private industry. This very feature is already triggering-off a whole series of implications that tend to undermine, rather than improve, indigenous farming structures. Then there are problems with the technology itself. Its focus is enormously deep, while at the same time extremely limited. New biotechnologists tend to describe their activities as multidisciplinary. Indeed, progress in the different fields in which this technology is applied is very much based on molecular biologists, geneticists, plant physiologists and scientists from other disciplines working together and integrating their research.

But it seems that this interdisciplinarity stops at the molecular and cellular level. The innovation is achieved with genes, cells and tissues, with the resulting plants or animals being the means to take the invention to the farmer's field. This reductionist approach is far narrower than that of the original biotechnologists who use hundreds of different strategies to obtain a whole range of different goals. One cannot help but wonder how an inserted gene or two would affect the complex integrated systems as developed by Third World farmers. This is not to say that traditional farming practices could not use a helping hand from modern science. They can, and in specific cases urgently need it. Peruvian farmers would very much welcome frost- and disease-tolerant potato varieties. The Sahelians could very well use better drought-tolerant millets, while Filipino upland rice farmers certainly would not mind having improved dry-land rice varieties at their disposal.

Often, though, the problem with some help is that it gets you out of a nasty situation only to cause a more profound one in the long run. The consequences of decades of massive food 'aid' is one example of such help. The problem with the help the new biotechnologies might offer is that it is based on an extremely narrow genetic focus. Just as the 'chemical-fix' resulted in the pesticide treadmill from which agriculture is still suffering, the narrow 'genetic-fix' of the new biotechnologies might also create greater problems than it solves. A new variety with resistance to drought or disease can be a real solution at the local level, but only if it fits into the prevailing farming practices, which can differ considerably in different locations. In that context, the isolation and transfer of a specific gene to solve a particular problem, is only the beginning. Other questions are, how the new variety performs in multiple cropping, does it retain traditional 'side' uses, how does it treat the soil, does it fit in the local labour scheme, and many, many more.

The strategy of the new biotechnologist to obtain better pest control, for example, consists basically of three elements. First, there is the typical tissue-culture work to obtain disease-free planting material. Secondly, genetic engineering is used to transfer pest and disease resistant genes to crops. Finally, there is the work on 'bio-pesticides' that might produce micro-organisms that combat pathogens. In Chapter 5 the dangers of uniform tissue-cultures, single gene resistance, and the narrow spectrum of current bio-pesticide research have already been pointed out. By comparison, indigenous farmers not only develop indigenous varieties to resist problems with pathogens, but also use rotation techniques, multiple cropping, botanical extracts, green manure, composting, and above all genetic diversity successfully to obtain healthy crops. Table 9.2 gives, in simplified form, some comparison of the different approaches in various areas.

Perhaps more than the science itself, it is the way in which it is being developed and the context within which it is brought to the market, which determine whether the new biotechnologies will strengthen, rather than destroy, sustainable agricultural practices. The recent history of technological change in Third World agriculture does not give too much hope. The Green Revolution's monocultural mind might have been responsible for spectacular increases in productivity of specific crops, but at the same time it undermined the basis of the productive system itself. This is largely due to the 'top-down' approach to science and development. The donors set the agenda, the IARCs developed the technology, regional and national

Table 9.2
Sustainable agriculture: farmers and biotech approaches

Problem	Biotech	Farmers
Pests & diseases	Single-gene resistance; engineered bio-pesticides	Genetic diversity; indigenous varieties; intercropping; insecticidal plants; crop rotation
Weeds	Herbicide tolerant genes	Early soil coverage; intercropping; cover crops; allelopathic crops
Water	Drought tolerant genes	Moisture conservation practices; contour ploughing; different varieties for different micro climates; water retaining associated crops (Vetiver grass, etc.)
Plant nutrients	Engineered nitrogen fixing crops and microbes	Soil conservation techniques; multiple cropping with legumes; integrated animal and crop agriculture (dung); composting; green manure
Soil degradation	Saline and other tolerance genes	Restore degraded soils (composting, green manure, rotation, etc.); avoid destruction of the soil in the first place
Yield	Yield increase for monocropping	Polycropping; one crop for multiple functions; use of associated crops and animals (weeds, fish, snails, etc.)

research institutes worked on it, after which armies of agriculture extension workers tried to persuade farmers to make use of it.

Although some of the research institutions are now trying to work more with farmers and their local organizations, the overall approach is predominantly unchanged. With the privatization of biotechnology putting the IARCs in the uncomfortable position of having to negotiate access to the technology in deals with TNCs, which can influence what it is used for, reorientation of the top-down approach seems difficult. The same might be said of those national biotechnology programmes that tend to focus on cash crops, export commodities and large-scale plantations, while at the same time ignoring local food production systems.

In trying to answer the question of how the new biotechnologies could benefit the rural poor, perhaps a useful start is to point to all the work that is *not* being done. Simple mass selection to improve local varieties is one example of under-supported research. Work on enhancing multiple cropping and rotation techniques, rationalization of the use of wild plants in local diets and the upgrading of traditional crop protection practices, are just a few others. With highly promising technical solutions being heralded at every possible occasion, the focus is often blurred. Yes, the new biotechnologies have something to offer, but so have small farmers themselves. Research oriented towards reinforcing the solid foundations of agricultural systems which have been developed for millennia is highly sporadic and seriously under-funded. At the same time, research on the quicker short-term and high-tech panaceas, which often result in the undermining of those foundations in the long-term, attract the imagination – and most of the money. Part of the reason is reductionist science itself. Incapable of grasping the immense complexity of entirety it turns its focus on minute parts of it, while still claiming solutions for the whole. Another reason, without doubt, is that money tends to go to places where it multiplies fast, which is often not in the fields of indigenous farmers. Be it a cause or a consequence, the farmer who is meant to benefit ends up being a target rather than a source.

Promoting people's participation

More direct involvement of farmers, community organizations and related NGOs in research and development of new solutions for agriculture has become the central theme at virtually every meeting on environment and/or development. But it might take a while before scientists and policy makers really manage to figure out how to implement this reverse strategy. Yet, turning the top-down approach rightside up seems the only viable way of ensuring sustainable development. Using biotechnology, and science in general, to improve and enhance the sustainable production systems of indigenous farmers, rather than replacing them with miracle solutions, should be the first priority. Part of the miracle is already there in the form of proven sustainable farming practices. It also exists in the form of the highly efficient working relationships of farmers' movements, community organizations and NGOs working at local, national or international levels. Examples are as numerous as they are diverse.

One of them might come from the Philippines. Home of IRRI, the institute that spearheaded the development of the Green Revolution's rice varieties, Filipino NGOs became acutely aware of the many negative consequences of the new rice technology. Working at the local level they started developing with farmers a unique system to collect, conserve, improve and reintroduce the indigenous rice varieties that have not yet been lost. Endowed with the name MASIPAG, the programme brings together NGOs, farmers' organizations and scientists. Between 1986 and 1988, 140 traditional rice varieties were collected, screened and improved, but work is also being carried out on bio-fertilizers, farming systems and training. The first results of this integrated approach were indigenous varieties yielding between 4.5 and 6.5 tonnes per hectare, which is more than even the best IRRI varieties. An important reason for starting to work together in MASIPAG, was the recognition that in the IRRI approach, farmers have no hand in the choice of the varieties to be released. Testing there is normally done under optimum rather than farmers' conditions, and the IRRI emphasis is on yield *per se* without due consideration of farmers' requirements, such as low inputs and nutrient quality. In the MASIPAG programme, farmers are active participants in all phases of the undertaking, including collection, evaluation and cross-breeding of the material.[24]

With the mounting recognition of the importance of genetic diversity and the role of small farmers, especially women, the approach described above is taken by an increasing number of NGOs, often with encouraging results. In Zimbabwe, where communal farmers make up over 70% of the farming community, the Zimbabwe Seeds Action Network (ZSAN) was launched, involving several NGOs and farmers' organizations in the collection, testing, multiplication and distribution of indigenous varieties of several crops. KENGO (Kenya Energy and Environment Organizations) has extensive experience with local seed conservation and agro-forestry schemes using indigenous varieties to arrest soil erosion. In Peru, NGOs are setting up small centres for the multiplication and distribution of disease-free local potato varieties. Sometimes with, but often without, funding from Northern agencies who, in turn, also become increasingly aware of the potential of working with local NGOs and small farmers, such initiatives deserve much broader attention.

But apart from fostering co-operation and direct involvement at the local level, NGOs have important functions at many other levels. One feature of many NGOs is their highly interactive way of working and communicating. Sometimes organized in national, regional or international networks, while in other cases relying on extensive bilateral contacts, the highly diverse NGO family can play an important role in influencing the way biotechnology is being used.

One important function is the monitoring of what research is being done and what impact it will have. NGOs participating in different networks often focus their attention on specific corporations, many of which are deeply involved in biotechnology. NGOs already contribute substantially to understanding the impact of biotechnology by monitoring ways in which the industry is being restructured, research priorities are set, which companies are dominating the market, trade and marketing practices of the companies involved, and so on. Another feature that all the issue networks have in common is an active participation of NGOs from both industrialized and developing countries. Also important is the differentiation in their expertise: some work at the local level, others are active in trying to change national policies, while yet others work more at lobbying international agencies. Co-operation in many of the existing issue-oriented networks ensures communication and the necessary flow of information. NGOs lobbying in the corridors of different UN bodies and other policy making institutions need the experience of those working at the local level, while grass-roots organizations might be helped with information more accessible to groups working at the international level.

International NGOs work in stimulating discussion on patents at WIPO, and encouraging Third World diplomats to take a stronger stand in that discussion. The same is true for debates about the changing trade relations arising from biotechnology in bodies like UNCTAD and GATT, and on labour aspects in the ILO. The impact of biotechnology on health and the environment is raised respectively within the World Health Organization and the UN Environment Programme (WHO and UNEP) and the impact on agricultural production at FAO. In many of these bodies the discussions are heavily dominated by the North because of lack of information, resources and expertise on the part of the developing countries. NGOs have often played a crucial role in bridging this gap by providing concrete and timely information to Third World delegates and by discussing strategies with them. The positions of Northern delegations can be influenced by mobilizing public opinion in industrialized countries and through direct contacts with national governments. In all cases, this work of what has become known as the Third System[25] is of utmost importance in shaping developments in biotechnology in such a way that those who need it most, benefit.

Notes and references

1. Quoted in Jack Doyle, 'The Agricultural Fix', in *Multinational Monitor*, February 1986, pp. 3–15.

2. Quoted in Jack Doyle, *Altered Harvest*, Viking, New York, 1985, p. 280.

3. Calestous Juma, *Biological Diversity and Innovation*, ACTS, Nairobi, 1989, p. 35.

4. Miguel Altieri, 'The Significance of Diversity in the Maintenance of the Sustainability of Traditional Agroecosystems', in *ILEIA Newsletter*, Vol. 3, No. 2, Leusden, July 1987, p.3.

5. Ibid.

6. Mogbuama example from Paul Richards, 'Spreading Risks Across Slopes: Diversified Rice Production in Central Sierra Leone', in *ILEIA Newsletter*, Vol. 3, No. 2, Leusden, July 1987.

7. Robert Rhoades, 'Thinking like a Mountain', in *ILEIA Newsletter*, Vol. 4, No. 1, Leusden, March 1988, p. 4.

8. Miguel Altieri, 1987, op. cit., p. 3.

9. Quoted in Albrecht Benzing, 'Andean Potato Peasants are Seed Bankers', in *ILEIA Newsletter*, Vol. 5, No. 4, Leusden, December 1989, p. 13.

10. Purna Chhetri, 'Bishnu's and Kheti's Sustainable Farm in Nepal', in *ILEIA Newsletter*, Vol. 4, No. 1, Leusden, March 1988.

11. 'Intercropping: Farming for the Future?' in *SPORE*, bulletin of CTA, No. 15, Wageningen, July 1988, p. 4.

12. Interview with T. Odhiambo, Director of ICIPE, in *ILEIA Newsletter*, Vol. 6, No. 1, Leusden, March 1990, p. 4.

13. Ibid.

14. Flores Milton, 'Velvetbeans: An Alternative to Improve Small Farmers' Agriculture', in *ILEIA Newsletter*, Vol. 5, No. 2, Leusden July 1989, pp. 8–9.

15. 'Intercropping: Farming for the Future?', 1988, op. cit., p.5.

16. Miguel Altieri, 1987, op. cit., p. 4.

17. 'Intercropping: Farming for the Future?', 1988, op. cit., p.5.

18. 'Tapping Farmers' Knowledge of Crop Protection', in *SPORE*, No. 26, Wageningen, April 1990, p. 12.

19. 'Sustainable Agricultural Production', in *SPORE*, No. 16, Wageningen, September 1988, p. 6.

20. 'Intercropping: Farming for the Future?', 1988, op. cit., p.5.

21. Jurgen Carls, 'Land-use Systems in Marginal Highland Areas', in *ILEIA Newsletter*, Vol. 4, No. 1, Leusden, March 1988, p. 10.

22. M. Altieri, 1987, op. cit., p. 6.

23. Purna Chhetri, 1988, op. cit., p. 16.

24. For a description of the MASIPAG programme, see 'Proceedings, Asian Regional Workshop on Plant Genetic Resources Conservation', Malang, 6–11 December 1987, *SEARICE*, Manila, 1988, pp. 70–1.

25. The Third System comprises NGOs and their networks, the first system being the governments and the second system the industry.

Epilogue

When I was about to finish this book, and in the process of the final checking of language, footnotes, sources and other little details, I allowed myself to escape a few days from the solitude of writing and accepted an invitation from the European Parliament to address a hearing on the patenting of life forms. I admit that I was not thoroughly prepared. Most of the preparations for my talk in Brussels took place in a cramped airplane seat on a flight that took less than two hours. Still, some of the reactions to my talk, in which I pointed to the negative implications of life patents, were breathtaking. Especially revealing were the reactive comments from the representatives of the European Commission. Berthold Schwab, leading the Commission's crusade for life patents, tried to convince the Parliament with arguments I thought nobody dared to use anymore. 'If we want to prevent half of the [world's] population from dying of starvation in the coming century, then we obviously cannot reach that objective with biological methods only', he exclaimed when reacting to comments that questioned some of the bright promises of biotechnology for developing countries. 'Of course, if you say we accept that several billion people are going to starve to death as a result of not accepting the patent system, then that is a position the European Commission cannot support', was his response to those criticizing the patenting of life forms.

On the plane back to Barcelona, I was not quite sure what to think. While the other invited experts who addressed the hearing had probably gone home with the firm conviction never to go back to Brussels again, I was still reflecting on the hysterical reactions from officials of a Commission which is supposed to be preparing the future of several hundred millions of Europeans. If pronounced by a speaker from any public interest group they would have definitely destroyed the credibility and fundraising potential of that organization in a flash.

The mere exclamation that we need biotechnology – and patents to promote it – as the only solution to the world's problems is still a message that many want to hear. When starting to write this book I was wondering whether the arguments against this view, written so many years ago, in which I insisted that biotechnology is not a solution but merely a tool, had not now become superfluous. One day's visit to Europe's future decision making body convinced me that such a message is still needed, especially for those who have the power to decide.

This book will undoubtedly be seen by some as biased. Maybe it is, in that it does focus more on the structural changes that the bio-revolution is provoking, than on the individual improvements that the new biotechnologies might bring to the farmer's field. Its analysis of how the technology is being controlled by industrialized countries and their corporations, and being used to transform the input and the output of today's agriculture to the detriment of the poor in the South, might be considered by some as too pessimistic. I sincerely hope it is, but I am not convinced.

What is perhaps most disturbing in the current approach of the new biotechnologists is the lack of recognition of the impressive contributions that the 'original' biotechnologists are already making. Throughout the book I have argued that these contributions should be taken as a starting point for scientific research, rather than its products just being taken as a basic raw material. Nevertheless, just as there are dangers in painting bright pictures of the potential of the new biotechnologies for the world's poor, romanticizing the practices of subsistence farmers should also be eschewed. Science – and biotechnology – can and should contribute together to the improvement of such farming systems, provided that the parameters of research are set on the basis of the local situation and in collaboration with farmers and their communities. This necessarily means that the resulting solutions will often be primarily of local significance, rather than automatically applicable at the global level.

Schwab's statement that the world's food problems are beyond solution with current biological techniques is an intriguing one. It insinuates that biotechnology is something separate from biology. It assumes that we now have this something much better than the good old life sciences. Most of all, it represents the viewpoint that universal solutions should be found for global problems. It was precisely this approach that made David Ehrenfeld, writing for *New Scientist*, exclaim:

> This is the age of generality; diversity is out of style. In biology, diversity held its own until the formulation of the central dogma of molecular biology: DNA makes RNA protein. From then diversity makes its descent into the second rate and the second class.[1]

Yet, today more than ever, the fourth resource and its diversity form the crucial cornerstone for survival. A biotechnology that expands on such diversity, rather than diminishing it, would be the type of tool welcome to farmers and consumers everywhere. Much of the outcome of the bio-revolution will depend on whether the public in general, and public institutions in particular, will retain or recover a voice in priority setting. *Biotechnology and the Future of World Agriculture* was written with the conviction that this is something worth fighting for.

Notes and references

1. Quoted in B. Edelman, M A. Hermitte (eds), 'L'Homme, la nature et le droit', Christian Bourgeois Editeur, 1988, pp. 282–3.

Index